MY RUSSIA
War or Peace?

Also by Mikhail Shishkin

Maidenhair
The Light and the Dark
Calligraphy Lesson: The Collected Stories

MY RUSSIA

War or Peace?

Mikhail Shishkin

Translated from the German by
Gesche Ipsen

riverrun

First published in Germany in 2019 under the title *Frieden oder Krieg*
by Verlagsgruppe Random House GmbH.
This translation first published in Great Britain in 2023 by

riverrun

An imprint of

Quercus Publishing Ltd
Carmelite House
50 Victoria Embankment
London EC4Y 0DZ

An Hachette UK company

A CIP catalogue record for this book is available
from the British Library

HB ISBN 978 1 52942 778 3
TPB ISBN 978 1 52942 779 0
EBOOK ISBN 978 1 52942 780 6

10 9 8 7 6 5 4 3 2 1

Typeset by CC Book Production
Printed and bound in Great Britain by Clays Ltd, Elcograf S.p.A.

Papers used by riverrun are from well-managed forests and other responsible sources.

Contents

Foreword to the English Edition

It hurts to be Russian.

When Vladimir Putin launched his 'special military operation' in Ukraine, he claimed that its aim was to save the Russians, Russian culture and the Russian language from Ukrainian fascists. In the process, it is predominantly the Russian-speaking cities in the east of the country, together with their populations, that have been wiped out. War crimes have been committed not only against people, but also against my language. The language of Alexander Pushkin and Leo Tolstoy, Marina Tsvetaeva and Joseph Brodsky has become the language of war criminals and murderers. For the foreseeable future, Russia will be associated not with Russian music and literature, but with bombs dropping on children and those terrible images from Bucha.

Moreover, the regime's criminal actions taint the whole of

the country. Monstrous crimes have been committed in the name of my people, my country, in my name. But there is another Russia. That other Russia is suffering pain and anguish. In the name of my Russia, in the name of my people, I would like to ask the Ukrainians for forgiveness – but I know that what has been happening in Ukraine is unforgivable.

When my father was eighteen, he went to the front to avenge his brother's murder at the hands of the Germans. After the war, he spent the rest of his life hating the Germans, and everything to do with the country. I told him, 'But Dad, Germany has some great literature! German is a beautiful language!' But my words had no effect on him. When this war is over, what will I be able to say to the Ukrainians, whose houses have been bombed and plundered by Russian soldiers, whose relatives have been killed by Russian missiles? That Russian literature is wonderful, and that Russian is such a beautiful language?

When war starts, culture has failed. Great German literature couldn't avert Auschwitz, great Russian literature couldn't prevent the Gulag, and my books and those of other Russian authors published in the past twenty years couldn't avert this tragedy.

So what can writers do? They can do what they do best – make themselves heard. They must tell it like it is. If you say nothing, you're effectively supporting the aggressor and the war. In the nineteenth century, the Poles fought against tsarist Russia 'for your and our freedom', and now the Ukrainians are fighting for your and our freedom. They are defending not only their human dignity, but the dignity of all humankind. Ukraine is defending our very freedom and dignity, and we must help in any way we can.

My mother was Ukrainian and my father was Russian; I can't help but be glad that they're not around to experience the tragedy that has hit our people.

This war hasn't only just begun. It began in 2014 – but the Western world refused to see it, and acted as if things weren't all that bad. In the intervening years, I've kept trying to explain to people who this Putin is, in my writings as well as in public appearances. It didn't work. Now Putin has explained it himself.

These chapters were originally published in German in 2019 (as part of *Frieden oder Krieg*, which included separate chapters written by the veteran TV journalist Fritz Pleitgen). As relevant as they were then, they are becoming more so each day, and the future I predict in the final chapters – what lies in store for Russia and for the rest of the world – has become our present. Back then, I wrote this:

> The glorious recovery of Crimea already has its own chapter in [Russian] school textbooks, and the next chapter waiting in the wings will tell the story of how Kyiv crawled on its knees back into the arms of the Russian world, like the prodigal son . . . the Kremlin will keep stoking the conflict in Donbas; sometimes it'll let it die down a little, sometimes it'll add fresh fuel to it . . . Putin will never give in.

On 24 February 2022, Russia's patience ran out. The Kremlin decided not to wait for Kyiv to come crawling back of its own accord. Since that day, the world has become a different place. The West has woken up. It has expanded what I described as the 'half-baked sanctions' that were in place in 2019, and banned, or substantially banned, Russian oil and gas imports; it has excluded Russian banks from SWIFT; in 2019, NATO was considering further expansion and thinking of admitting Finland and Sweden – as a result of this year's events, the two countries are in fact close to joining (at the time of writing, only Turkey and Hungary are yet to ratify their membership). Yet the West still finds Russia inexplicable and disconcerting, and the purpose of my book remains unchanged: I want to disclose my country to Western readers, to explain Russia and its past, present and future. It is also a love letter to my country, which is blessed with stunning nature and wonderful culture, yet keeps turning into a monster that devours its own and other countries' children.

The aim of Russia's 'special military operation' is to destroy democratic Ukraine. The result of the 'special military operation' will be the destruction of Putin's Russia. But what then?

Two previous attempts to introduce democracy in Russia have both failed. The first Russian democracy of 1917 lasted only a few months; the one of the 1990s just managed to cling on for a few years. Each time my country tries to build a democratic society and to institute elections, a parliament and a republic, it finds itself back in a totalitarian empire. Again and again, Russian history bites its own tail.

Do dictatorships and dictators give birth to an enslaved population, or does an enslaved population give birth to dictatorships and dictators? It's the old chicken-and-egg conundrum. How can the vicious circle be broken? Where can Russia make a fresh start?

If Hitler's Germany was able to extricate itself from the vicious circle of dictatorship and slave mentality, why shouldn't Russia? The Germans have diligently studied the topics 'Dealing with the Past' and 'Processing Guilt', and managed to create a democratic society; yet Germany's rebirth was founded on its total, crushing military defeat. Russia, too, needs its zero hour. It cannot make a fresh start as a democracy without repentance and an acknowledgement of national guilt.

Russia was never de-Stalinised, and there were no Nuremberg trials for the Communist Party. Russia's fate now depends on its de-Putinisation. Just as, in 1945, the Germans who 'didn't know' were confronted with the concentration camps, the Russians who 'don't know' have to be confronted with ruined Ukrainian cities and the bodies of dead children. We Russians must openly and bravely acknowledge our guilt and ask for forgiveness. Every Russian has to go down this road. But will Russia get down on its knees in Kyiv, Kharkiv and Mariupol, or anywhere that Russian tanks have been: in Budapest, Prague, Tallinn, Vilnius, Riga, Grozny?

In 1945, the Germans tried to justify themselves, arguing

that, yes, Hitler was a vile and evil criminal, but they, the German people, didn't know anything about it – that they, too, were Hitler's victims. The moment the Russians use the same argument, and claim that Putin's criminal gang took the people hostage, that he did wage a criminal war against Ukraine, but ordinary Russians didn't know that and thought it was about liberating the Ukrainians from fascists, that they, too, were Putin's victims – the moment this happens, de-Putinisation will fail, and a new Putin will be born.

Neither NATO nor the Ukrainians can do the de-Putinising for the Russians. The Russian people must clean up the country themselves. Are we up to the task? Is it realistic to expect constitutional democracies to form in those territories that will declare their independence from Moscow – since the disintegration of the Russian empire isn't over yet? Yugoslavia showed how quickly a multinational state can descend into brutal war and genocide, and if violence escalates in Russia it will set my country back centuries. For the West, this would mean a fresh wave of countless refugees.

A new era of turmoil is on the horizon for Russia, where most people have lost faith in democratic ideas and are pinning their hopes on a strongman ruler. Such a strongman will no doubt be found, and the West, too, will understand and accept a new 'dictatorship of order'. No one wants turmoil in a country that has lots of rusty nuclear missiles.

This is my credo: there must be an acknowledgement of national guilt. Without complete de-Putinisation, Russia has no future. A long and painful process of rebirth is its only option, and all those sanctions, the poverty, being ostracised, will be the least of Russia's worries. For the Russian people not to undergo an inner rebirth – that would be far more terrible. Putin is a symptom, not the disease.

It should now be the mission of Russian writers and artists to show the world that there is another Russia, and that not all Russians support this war. This war isn't being waged between Ukrainians and Russians, but between human beings who speak both Ukrainian and Russian on the one hand, and inhuman beings who speak the language of lies and are willing to obey criminal orders on the other. In this war, then, there are no nationalities – only human beings and inhuman ones. The latter have no nationality, because they are this criminal regime's slaves, who beat up and arrest the humans who are taking to Russia's streets to protest against the war.

Putin's crime is that he has poisoned the people with hate. Putin will step down at some point, but the pain and hate will probably remain in their souls for a long time. Then it will be up to culture, to literature and the arts, to process the trauma. The day a dictator ends his miserable, unworthy life, doesn't mark the end of culture – it never has and never will. There will be no need for books about Putin or books that explain the war: war, someone ordering the people of one nation to kill those of another, cannot be explained. True literature defies war. True literature is about our need for love, not hate.

A reader once told me, 'Your book prevented my love for

Russia from suffocating in the blood of the Ukrainians.' The Russian army's invasion of Ukraine has caused so much bloodshed – can a book still prevent anyone's love for Russia from drowning in all that blood?

After war comes anti-war literature. Just like Ernest Hemingway and Erich Maria Remarque once, I have no doubt that there will be young authors writing about their experiences in this war. Both Russians and Ukrainians will write books, and they'll be very different books. Both will write about the pain that loss brings, about death, about grief; but while Ukrainian literature will see books on the birth of a free country, the heroic resistance against evil and the fight for human dignity, Russian authors will be preoccupied with the acknowledgement of national guilt for the crimes that have been committed.

Hate is a disease. Culture is the cure.

Chapter 1

The Paradox of the Lie

I sometimes think it's the words that are the problem.

As they cross the Russian border, some words turn out to be mislabelled crates, their contents either quietly, eerily exchanged or simply stolen. Against a Russian backdrop, the best, most wonderful terms lose their meaning.

When I was young, it all seemed so straightforward: our country had been taken over by a communist gang; if we ejected the party, the borders would open and we'd once again become part of the global family of nations that lived according to the rules of democracy and freedom, and honoured the rights of the individual. 'Parliament', 'republic', 'constitution', 'elections' – the words had a fairy-tale aura about them. We were naive back then, and somehow it never occurred to us that those words already existed in Russia: after all, the 1936

Stalin Constitution was 'the most democratic constitution in the world'. We already lived among those weighty words that were crammed into all the papers, and had regular elections too.

We forgot that the good Western words that had crossed the border and penetrated our society had lost their original meaning; that they had begun to describe all kinds of things, except what they actually meant.

The constitution guaranteed all sorts of rights; there they were, in black and white: 'the universal and equal right to a direct vote' – 'freedom of speech, freedom of the press, freedom of assembly and the holding of mass meetings, the freedom of street processions and demonstrations' – 'Citizens of the USSR are guaranteed inviolability of the person. No person may be placed under arrest except by decision of a court or with the sanction of a procurator' – 'The inviolability of the homes of citizens and privacy of correspondence are protected by law'.

This wonderful constitution was written by Nikolai Bukharin. Three months after it was adopted, in March 1937, its author was arrested for espionage and plotting to assassinate Stalin. In his final letter, Bukharin begged Stalin to allow him to take a fatal dose of morphine rather than be shot. Instead of granting him that mercy, the NKVD chief Nikolai Yezhov – who personally oversaw Bukharin's execution – forced the condemned man to wait his turn and look on as his fellow prisoners were shot dead before him.

Bukharin married three times. His first wife, Nadezhda Lukina, was arrested on 1 May 1938 and shot on 9 March 1940.

His second wife, Esfir Gurvich, and their daughter Svetlana spent years in the Gulag. His third wife, Anna Larina, was also arrested. Their son Yuri grew up in an orphanage, not knowing who his parents were.

The words had abandoned their author. It seems as if the words conspired against us.

The simplest, most common words can mean very different things in Russia. When Russians talk about the market economy or private ownership, it sounds appealing and familiar to Western ears. But it's an illusion. In Russia, there is no guaranteed private ownership, no market economy in the Western sense. Or take the state: in the civilised world, the state has long been considered an instrument whose function is to act in its citizens' interests, not its own; it is built from the bottom up, and authority is delegated upwards only for things not within the competence of the lower strata; and the separation of the legislative, executive and judicial branches of government is instilled in every citizen from infancy. In Russia, however, the state means something very different. It means power and territory – and both are sacrosanct. In the West, a state's citizens are its shareholders; in Russia, no matter whose coat of arms hangs over the gates, they are the state's serfs.

Who in the Soviet Union would have thought that, although the Communist Party would disappear, in the new Russia all those good words like 'democracy', 'parliament' and 'constitution' would turn into mere cudgels in a never-ending battle for power and money?

Take the word 'democracy': in Europe, it guarantees personal freedom and human rights. For most Russians, it signifies the chaos of the 1990s, and no one wants to see the country return to the 'wild nineties'.

In Russia and the West, the same words can trigger vastly different reactions. In the West, for instance, we smile at the now-famous statement that the Soviet Union's break-up was the 'greatest geopolitical catastrophe of the twentieth century' (Putin, April 2005). Yet whereas the US and western Europe saw the end of the Soviet Union as a victory for freedom and democracy, the majority of Russians saw it as a large-scale human and social catastrophe. When Putin said this, he echoed the sentiments of most Russians.

Probably the greatest source of misunderstanding between Russia and the West is the fact that in Russia, democratic terms are just empty, inconsequential shells. Western governments are assessed against them, but in Russia they are facades, and everybody knows that behind these facades is nothing but yawning emptiness. The Russian state can proclaim 'laws', a 'constitution', 'human rights' and all kinds of 'freedoms', but Russia lives, as it has always done, according to one rule only: whatever the all-powerful Kremlin says goes. This is why, for example, my country's government simply cannot understand why Britain doesn't extradite Chechen separatists to Russia. The way they see the world, the matter could be sorted with a phone call from the British PM to the judge in charge of the case.

In the Russian universe, big words work differently: they serve as camouflage. What to an outsider looks like a lie merely facilitates everyday conversation between Russian speakers. This is not a paradox – it's the Russian reality of words.

'There are no Russian troops in Crimea,' Putin told the world in spring 2014 with a sly grin. People in the West didn't understand why Putin would so blatantly lie to his people. But the people didn't think of it as lying. Their attitude was, 'Everyone deceives their enemy, we get it. Deceiving the enemy isn't a sin, it's a military virtue.' And how proudly did Putin later admit that, yes, Russian troops *had* been active in Crimea!

Russia brazenly lied to the West when it claimed that it didn't shoot down the Boeing 777 over Donetsk. Everyone knows it's a lie. And then life goes on – business as usual.

As Putin brazenly dishes up patent lies to Western politicians, he watches their reaction with evident interest and not without amusement; he basks in their bewilderment and helplessness. Brazenness is a display of strength, and puts your opponent on the spot. The next move is theirs; but they don't know what to do, because they aren't prepared to lie like that. Western politicians don't lie openly – when they do lie, they do it as surreptitiously as possible. In democratic Europe, lying is governed by a different algorithm.

In his memoirs, Chris Patten, the last governor of Hong Kong and former EU commissioner, recalls sitting next to Putin during a summit. They were discussing Chechnya, and the human rights violations that had occurred there. 'It was odd . . . We knew that Putin was lying. He knew that we knew he was lying. He did not give a damn, and we all let him get away with it'.*

The Kremlin claims it isn't involved in the war in eastern Ukraine, and everyone knows that this, too, is a lie, but the Western diplomats put up with it. The Kremlin sends soldiers to eastern Ukraine, allows them to die there in this nefarious sham intervention, and afterwards lies to their families about how and where they died. The families pretend to believe the government, and say nothing. When Putin lies in his own country, everyone knows he's lying and he knows that everyone knows, but his voters consent to his lies. Russian truth is a never-ending lie.

None of this is new. Soviet Radio once broadcast the following lie: 'TASS [the Soviet news agency] says that there are no Soviet troops on Korean territory.' There were no Soviet troops in Egypt, Algeria, Yemen, Syria, Angola, Mozambique, Ethiopia, Cambodia, Bangladesh or Laos either. If the soldiers stationed in those places were lucky enough to survive and return home, they were warned not to talk about it. Their own country disavowed them. It was only in the 1990s that the state belatedly acknowledged their service and expanded the 'Federal Law on Veterans' to include the military actions they were involved in. The law lists every war that our soldiers

---

* Chris Patten, *Not Quite the Diplomat: Home Truths About World Affairs* (London: Penguin, 2005), p. 202.

and officers have fought – wars that our various governments nonetheless categorically and angrily denied having had any part in. Future legislators will have to add Ukraine to the list.

Russia has returned to the Soviet days of the total lie. Back then, those in power signed a social contract with their subjects that would guide life in Russia for decades: 'We know that we're lying and that you're lying, and we'll keep on lying to survive.' Generations of Russians have grown up under this social contract.

I once borrowed the children's book *Gelsomino in the Land of Liars* by Gianni Rodari from the school library. It tells the story of a boy who arrives in a country that has been hijacked by pirates, who are now forcing everyone to lie. They order the cats to bark and the dogs to miaow, bread is now called 'ink', all of the money in circulation is counterfeit, and a paper called *The Model Liar* is the inhabitants' source for any important news. The absurdity of the situation amused me, of course, but the reason the book enjoyed such huge success among adults is that they, unlike their children, knew which country Rodari was really writing about. It was Orwell for beginners. I remember my parents wondering why the book hadn't been banned – they knew that its hijacked country of lies was really their own.

Lies were everywhere. The newspapers, TV and teachers lied. The state hoodwinked its citizens and the citizens hoodwinked the state. Those were the rules of the game, and everyone knew what they were. We got used to them from nursery school onwards; this landscape of lies is where the movers and shakers who represent modern Russia grew up. For decades, the state lied to its own people and to foreigners, and nobody cared that no one believed each other. Soviet government posters told the people that the USSR was a 'bastion of freedom', even as it sent its tanks all over the world. It invaded Czechoslovakia under the pretext that it had been 'invited' by 'a group of comrades' (a laughably small group – five functionaries from the Czech Communist Party's Stalinist wing). They lied when they claimed that we had been 'asked' to send troops to Afghanistan. They lied about plane crashes too, provided that no football or ice hockey teams died in them; after all, such tragedies only happen over there, in the West. When Leonid Brezhnev became general secretary of the Communist Party he lied to the whole world, erasing Nikita Khrushchev from official photos taken at a Red Square reception held in honour of Yuri Gagarin after he returned from space. They lied about the past, the present and the future no matter what the occasion, however important or trivial.

On TV, they joyfully reported that the five-year plan had been met, but in the shops the shelves emptied as the queues outside grew ever longer. We were living in a country where socialism had 'won', and the law said that the people owned everything; in reality, they owned nothing. In fact, no one owned anything. We were living in an extraordinary country full of slaves, where everyone belonged to the system – even our leaders.

The state demanded enthusiastic reports of successes in

all areas of the economy, and the reports it received from the people were jubilant and fake. The powers that be ordered a pack of lies, got it, and then pretended to believe those lies. Should anyone be unwilling to join in this word game, they were neutralised, censured, fired, arrested, killed. The severity of the punishment depended on the temperature of the time – in Stalin's day, they shot you. You'd better tell lies like everyone else, then, especially if you have a family and children to take care of.

My mother was a schoolteacher, but I was too young back then to appreciate how tough it was for her and the other teachers to plan their lessons. They faced an impossible task: teach the children to tell the truth, but also prepare them for life in the land of lies. The written rules stipulated that you should always tell the truth; but the unwritten rules said that if you told the truth, the consequences were your responsibility.

Our teachers loved us and wanted to save us, so they taught us lies they didn't believe themselves. They were afraid to say the wrong thing, but afraid for us even more than for themselves. A deadly word game was being played in our country. You had to say the right words while avoiding the dangerous ones, and although there was no official line separating the two, deep inside everyone knew where it was. Dissidents broke the rules of the game out of a suicidal sense of personal honour (as Aleksandr Solzhenitsyn famously urged people, 'Live not by lies'); the fearless young broke the rules too, because of their inexperience, and the teachers tried to save those truth-loving adolescents by vaccinating them with an invigorating dose of fear. The injection hurt a little, but it would protect them for the rest of their lives. Our English or Chemistry lessons may not have been the best, but we received an exemplary education in the difficult art of survival: we learnt how to say one thing, think another and do a third. A split personality, a cleaved consciousness – saying one thing while thinking and acting otherwise – shaped the reality of an entire nation. When a lie becomes detached from itself, it is capable of constructing a brand-new reality; and we are that reality. Every one of us Russians alive today is born of this false reality, both those who support the government and those who oppose it. You can't even call it a reprehensible lie, because all our vital force and instinct for survival are concentrated in it. You need certain qualities to maintain your will to survive behind the barbed wire of this prison camp called Russia. The structure of your psyche changes. This is not without consequences, especially when the qualities needed to survive are passed down through generations – generations for whom lies have been the elixir of life. In 'The Paradox of the Lie', his 1939 article about the dictatorships of Hitler and Stalin, the émigré philosopher Nikolai Berdyaev wrote that 'the people live in fear, and lies are the weapon with which they defend themselves'. We were all scared, and needed a way to defend ourselves! The state was afraid of its own people, so it lied; and the people participated in that lie, because they were afraid of the state. The lie thus safeguarded the existence of a society built on violence and fear.

You were supposed to lie, but not to believe. If you believed, you were soon lost. I still remember how we found out about Chernobyl: I was working at a school then, and one break-time a visibly agitated Physics teacher came into the staffroom to tell us what had happened. An acquaintance had told him about the tragedy on the quiet. We instantly believed him. It was he, not the government, who prompted us to quickly get the children back inside, so that they wouldn't be exposed to the radiation. For a long time, the official channels remained tight-lipped. Then, later, they reported on the events, but at the same time reassured us that we weren't in any danger whatsoever. We knew right away what it meant: if they said there was no danger, things had to be really bad.

Western politicians have a different relationship with lies. Western voters, too, think some of their politicians are liars and frauds – and for good reasons; and their lies can also have grave consequences, such as the one about Saddam Hussein's weapons of mass destruction. When compared to Russian autocrats, however, those politicians, who are subsequently divested of their power in the next election, look like small-time crooks. Can you imagine a US president or a British prime minister sending their troops into action, and washing their hands of them afterwards? The voters would never understand or forgive them for it.

Western politicians, whose fate is decided in the polling booth, need to say what they really mean if they want to win the voters' trust. In a democratic society, being caught in a lie can end a politician's career. The idea that you should take responsibility for your words has its roots in the fundamental transformation of European thought during the Reformation. The words you speak are taken seriously and considered binding; a civilised society is based on trust – trust in state institutions, and trust in the spoken word.

The different ways in which words function can be illustrated by the example of the two politicians who made the twentieth century the bloodiest in human history: Hitler and Stalin. When a Russian reads Hitler's repellent book, they see a sincerity and directness that would have been unimaginable from Stalin. Hitler's openly articulated hatred of the Jews stands in stark contrast to the Soviet rhetoric of 'the solidarity of the people'. This is where two different traditions collide: taking responsibility for what you say, and abusing words to camouflage what you actually mean. The Führer's candid words expressed real conviction, which earned him the trust of the German masses. He didn't lie to the Germans and, once in power, did what he promised he would do: he enacted the Nuremberg Race Laws, and thereby created the legal basis for the persecution of Jews. Anti-Semitism was now legitimate and legally prescribed; as in word, so in deed. Hitler's candid hate speech thus paved the way for the Holocaust. Stalin, however, never said a single word against the Jews in public, but he ordered the execution of members of the Jewish Anti-Fascist Committee after the war and instigated the nationwide persecution of Jews under the guise of fighting 'international

Zionism'; the notorious trial of the alleged 'Doctors' Plot' conspirators was meant to provide the pretext for a Soviet version of the 'Final Solution' – they had already started preparing for the deportation of Jews to Siberia along the same lines as previous deportations of other peoples. (Stalin's death put a stop to those plans.)

Both Gestapo agents and NKVD agents were executioners; but while the Gestapo tortured prisoners to get them to admit the truth, that they were a communist or a Jew, the NKVD tortured prisoners to extract a lie from them, to force them to falsely confess that they were a British-Japanese spy or an agent of international Zionism.

From podiums and in newspapers, they proclaimed that all ethnicities were equal in the Soviet Union and eulogised the country as a brotherhood of nations, but a covert state-sponsored anti-Semitism prevailed even decades after Stalin's death. The government may not have passed a law making it illegal for certain colleges and universities to accept Jewish students, but it was an unwritten law that everyone obeyed. In my country, you don't need official 'Nuremberg Race Laws'. The relationship between word and reality works differently here – which is why there's a grave misconception among Western political leaders when it comes to Russia: Western media and politicians try to judge the regime in Moscow by the things it says, to draw important political conclusions from statements made by the occupants of the Kremlin. But those statements merely translate as: 'We are lying and you know it, but you'll have to swallow our lie.' They judge Russian leaders by their words, whereas they should judge them by their actions.

Will Europe find a way to resist this tsunami of lies, or will it accept Putin's social contract?

If you want to understand Russia, you have to uncover the conspiracy of words. You have to compile a dictionary of misleading words, find the true, hidden meaning of mendacious, hackneyed terms, translate forgery into clarity. Every translator knows those so-called 'false friends', foreign words that resemble words in your own language and therefore seem familiar and unambiguous, but which actually mean something entirely different. When it comes to the Russian world, it seems that almost every word is a false friend – and if you don't clear up this muddle of words, all that talk about 'the mysterious country on the edge of civilisation' will never stop. People keep writing about the 'inscrutable Russian soul' – epitomised by Churchill's comment that Russia is 'a riddle wrapped in a mystery inside an enigma' – but Russians are neither puzzling nor mysterious. There are no 'puzzling and mysterious' people on this planet. There is only ignorance. In *The Frigate 'Pallada'*, an account of his voyage around the world, Ivan Goncharov – the famous author of *Oblomov*, the magnum opus of the 'psychology of the Russian soul' – remarked that the 'puzzling' Japanese 'think our politeness rude, and vice versa'. It was wrong, he said, to judge the inhabitants of Japan by European standards. In order to understand the Japanese mentality, their way of life and their politics, you had to know the country's history: 'No matter how well you know the human heart, no matter how much you have seen of life, it is difficult to follow the local customs if you don't have the key to the people's world view, morality and conventions. It is like trying to learn a language without a grammar or dictionary.'

Japanese, German, Papuan, Russian – we are all puzzling. But these puzzles can be solved. The past has provided the building blocks for our present.

We, the living generation, are a glove, and our history is the hand.

Chapter 2

The Mountain Tsar

When I was a kid, we used to play a game called 'Mountain Tsar' in winter. We'd pile up a mountain of snow in the yard and make a sort of icy slide down one side, and the aim was to climb to the top and push everyone else off by any means, fair or foul. Russian history has been playing this game for a thousand years now. The only difference is that, in this version, blood is shed, and sometimes inundates the entire country.

Alexander Herzen once said about writers: 'We are not the physicians, we are the pain.' He also devastatingly diagnosed life in Russia as ruled by a 'state that has installed itself in Russia like an occupying army'.

The fact that the state behaves like an occupying force towards its own people goes all the way back to the Vikings, whose invasion of what was then Slavic tribal territory marks the beginning of Russian history. Chroniclers have tried to prettify the event with the legend that the Vikings had been 'invited' by the Slavs, but the truth is that they conquered them. They founded a state there, just as they had previously done in Normandy and Sicily, settling in Novgorod and Kyiv. In 882, Prince Oleg made Kyiv the capital of his realm, which is why historians call the first major East Slavic state 'Kievan Rus'. The Slavs who rose up against the foreign intruders were brutally massacred; when the avaricious prince Igor the Old was killed by the Drevlians during one of his predatory raids, his widow Olga avenged his death by having five thousand Drevlians murdered on his burial mound and a delegation of their men burnt alive in a bath house. Iskorosten, the Drevlian capital, was reduced to ashes and the citizens mercilessly executed. The gulf between the ruler and the people was Russia's birth trauma.

The fact that the Scandinavian princes married Slavs and their children learnt to speak the local language did not affect their relationship to their subjects; later generations continued to live off raids, on foreign soil as well as in their own 'hunting ground', and the country fragmented into several rival principalities whose rulers treated the 'lowly masses' as prey, rather than fellow tribesmen.

Religion might have become a unifying factor, but the state's adoption of the Christian faith degenerated into yet another violation of the terrorised populace. According to the oldest surviving historical source, the *Primary Chronicle*, Prince Vladimir's choice between Islam, Judaism, Roman Catholicism and Byzantine Orthodoxy was guided by aesthetic principles; and he chose Orthodoxy, because his emissaries returned from 'Tsargrad' (i.e. Constantinople) with ecstatic accounts of an Orthodox service they attended at the Hagia Sophia, which was apparently so beautiful that it left them wondering whether they were 'still on earth or already in Heaven'. In truth, though, it was all a power play. The Byzantine empire was the mightiest in the region, and Vladimir chose Orthodox Christianity because he wanted to cosy up to the Byzantine imperial court. Russia's faith was determined by geopolitics.

In 998, the freshly converted ruler threw Kyiv's heathen idols into the Dnipro, and ordered the citizens to get themselves baptised in the river's waters. Refusal was punishable by death. That is how Christ's teachings arrived in Russia – and the prince's military retinue, the *druzhina*, employed brutal force as they performed compulsory baptisms in all corners of the realm.

Russia's Christianisation via Constantinople had fatal consequences for its history. Unlike the Roman Catholic Church, which insisted on Latin as the sole language of liturgy, the Orthodox Church gave Russians 'Old Church Slavonic', a language invented especially for the South Slavs by two Byzantine scholars, the brothers Cyril and Methodius – thus preventing the East Slavs from linking up with the culture of antiquity and excluding them from the developments taking place in Europe. Latin was the artery that brought civilisation to Europe, the language of science, medicine and law, the lingua franca of the

Church. While a supposedly dead language proved a vitalising force for western Europe, the Russians had a dead and fictitious Church language that remained mummified for centuries and contributed nothing to knowledge or social progress. It is not least for linguistic reasons that the Renaissance, the Reformation and the Enlightenment passed them by.

A lethal external threat like the thirteenth-century Mongolian invasion could have helped to unify the people, could have presented a historic opportunity for the rulers and the masses to overcome the gulf between them as they faced impending doom. But it didn't turn out that way. In fact, the Mongol invasion and the Rus's subsequent incorporation into the Golden Horde only deepened the chasm between the rulers and the people, turning it into an immutable constant in Russian politics.

Under Batu Khan, the Mongols founded the khanate of the Golden Horde, and in 1242 erected their capital, Sarai, on the lower reaches of the Volga. From that point on, the Rus belonged to the Golden Horde and Sarai was the Russian capital. The Rus was now an 'ulus' – a province – of the Mongolian empire, and the khan granted Russian princes control over their estates by means of a *yarlyk*, a gracious decree. The princes had to travel to Sarai to pay homage to the khan, and they and their retinue would prostrate themselves before him and kiss his feet. The Mongols refrained from stationing their own army on the occupied lands. Rather, it was the task of the Russian princes, as representatives of the khan, to exact tribute from the people. They were the tax collectors, defending the interests of the Golden Horde, and since their own lives depended on tributes, they behaved like occupiers in their own country. Mercilessly robbing the citizens of their own towns and villages was their survival strategy: so long as you did the khan's bidding, you might live another day. The Mongols did not need to get involved at all, because the various princes did not trust one another, and would denounce each other to the khan in Sarai. As far as their own subjects were concerned, however, the princes represented the Golden Horde, and while the rulers shared the people's language and religion, they still acted like enemy forces. This is how, right from the first, the Mongol occupation turned into an occupation of the people by the people's own rulers. The Tatar yoke was actually a Russian yoke.

In the Russian ulus, the rules of the game were the same as in the rest of the Mongolian empire. The khan considered the enslaved territories and people his property, and the law of violence did duty as the constitution of the realm. At their courts, the Russian princes imitated life in the capital of the Golden Horde, and the entire top-down power structure functioned according to the principle that you bowed upwards, and kicked downwards. The one key difference in the relationship between the people and those in power before and after the Mongol conquest was that, now, the princes were slaves too. To ensure its survival, the Russian political elite had acquired a slave mentality.

Alexander Nevsky, one of the founding fathers of the Russian state, is depicted in Sergei Eisenstein's eponymous Stalin-era cult film as a passionate patriot and popular folk hero, partly for having excelled in his youth as a remarkably courageous military leader. However, the reality is a little different. After Batu Khan conferred the Grand Duchy of Vladimir, the capital of northern Rus, on Alexander's brother Andrei, Andrei plotted an uprising against the Mongols and attempted to forge an alliance of princes against the ruler in Sarai. Yet Alexander spent a lot of time at the Great Khan's court in Sarai, where he schemed against his brother until Batu deposed Andrei and conferred the title of Grand Duke on Alexander. Alexander then led a punitive expedition against the Rus at the head of the Mongolian forces, which wiped out his brother's army, forcing Andrei to flee to Sweden. In 1257, when the Mongols conducted a census in advance of levying taxes, the citizens of Novgorod revolted, and Alexander once again led the Mongol forces into action, breaking the rebels' resistance with a vicious punitive campaign. Thousands had their noses cut off and their eyes gouged. The era of the Tatar yoke therefore began not when the Mongols invaded Russia, but when Alexander rose to power. It began with a Russian prince, who became the foreign occupier's vicious and effective enabler. Yet this didn't prevent the Orthodox Church from canonising Alexander Nevsky. He remains a Russian national hero to this day.

The *yarlyk* that bestowed the title of Grand Duke on the rulers of Moscow was the next milestone on the road to a

Russian state that 'installed itself like an occupying army'. Anyone who bore that title was the khan's viceroy, responsible for collecting tributes throughout the ulus. The Muscovite prince Ivan Kalita acquired the title in the fourteenth century, after a vicious fight with his rivals, having gained the Great Khan's trust by helping the Mongol army crush a rebellion in Tver, creating a bloodbath and laying waste to the entire principality. Ivan's loyalty to the khan and willingness to use brutal force against his own people augmented his power, and that of Moscow, his grand duchy. The Rus metamorphosed into the Golden Horde's Moscow ulus, its sovereignty made official by the relocation of the metropolitan's seat from Vladimir to Moscow. Grand Duke Ivan amassed his riches by lining his pockets with the lion's share of the tributes he collected all over the country. This is how he gained his nickname: Kalita means 'moneybags'. The ruler and the people were henceforth inextricably linked by violence and mutual fear, and the pattern of behaviour for Moscow's future rulers was born.

Over time, the Golden Horde fragmented, and out of the various power struggles in the disintegrating empire Moscow emerged as the strongest ulus. The Great Khan's viceroy was now a hereditary ruler. Yet when it came to social relationships, only one thing changed in the Moscow ulus: the land and the people, hitherto the property of the Great Khan, now belonged to the grand duke, who called himself 'tsar'. Moscow couldn't free itself from the Golden Horde, since you can't liberate yourself from yourself. Instead, it became a new Sarai; the

Tatar yoke – which never was a Tatar yoke, since the Mongols did not oppress the people themselves but delegated the task to compliant Russian princes – was over. What remained was the ulus, as a political system and as a mentality.

In the fifteenth century, Moscow appeared on the international stage as an independent player, and needed to assert itself against its Catholic neighbours in the West. Orthodox Christianity became its battle flag. The Church lent the tsarist empire that was waging war against every one of its neighbours its intellectual backing, and obligingly created a messianic military ideology. The new rulers' growing self-confidence transformed into a missionary zeal, and Moscow became the Third Rome. The fall of Byzantium left Russia as the only remaining independent state governed by the Orthodox faith. The Grand Duchy of Moscow was regarded as the earthly likeness of the kingdom of heaven, and as a state founded on truth. As the monk Filofei of Pskov famously said, 'Look and take care, pious Tsar, all the Christian empires have perished and together have passed over into your one empire. For two Romes have fallen, but the third is here, and there will be no fourth.'

With that, the Russian world was perfect. While the Renaissance and Reformation fired the imagination of the Europeans, a military empire rose in the east which treated its own people as soldiers. Ever since, autocracy and accord have provided the coordinates for Russian life, and victory over its enemies has been the country's sole aim. When you are at war with the rest of the world, expansion is your best defence; the only point of an individual's life is therefore to serve the Russian realm. Dying for the fatherland means supreme bliss. You don't choose the commanders and you don't question orders, and the mere suggestion of personal initiative, the mere flicker of a free thought, amounts to mutiny. Any expression of discontent, no matter how justified, is an act of treason. There are two kinds of people: ours (*nashi*) and foreigners. The foreigners hate us Russians, and it is their life's goal to destroy Russia. And the Russian god is the only god.

Private ownership, an essential concept in European societies, doesn't apply here: a Russian subject's life and property are but part of the country's strategic military reserves, and may at any moment be sacrificed to a higher cause. Loyalty to your superiors is both source and guarantor of all property. There is only one kind of property – the state's – and disloyalty leads to dispossession. There is no stable legal system, no concept of independent courts. The strongest own everything. The legacy of the Golden Horde survives in the 'legitimacy of the *yarlyk*', which is the legitimacy of violence.

The only thing that can protect people from the whims of the powerful is an unyielding supreme power. It guarantees order in the realm, and if the ruling power were to betray any weakness, the whole top-down power structure would fall apart and chaos would spread. This is why the people want a strongman ruler. Between chaos and order, everyone always chooses the latter. In Russia, no one wants a weak tsar; they want a tyrant.

The legend of Dracula (Vlad III, voivode of Wallachia) enjoyed great popularity in the fifteenth and sixteenth centuries. The western European versions only focused on his cruelty, but its Russian interpretation – *Skazanie o Drakule voevode* ('Stories of the voivode Dracula'), thought to have been written by the Russian diplomat Fyodor Kuritsyn – differs strikingly from the better-known Dracula legends. In Western representations, Dracula appears as a bloodthirsty despot, a manic sadist, a desecrator, executioner, demon and outright villain. In the Russian version, he is first and foremost an Orthodox ruler defending the one true religion against Muslim enemies of the faith, who maintains order in his realm; and because this mighty warrior's enemies are afraid to attack him, he is able to secure lasting peace. No one dares to steal anything, because everyone is afraid of the punishment. Officials don't accept bribes, because they tremble at the prospect of being impaled. The butcher as ideal ruler. *Skazanie o Drakule voevode* was the first original secular Russian book. The fact that of the many topics fashionable in Europe at the time it was this particular one that was sought after by Moscow's society, and that it was reinterpreted so radically, speaks volumes. The book was enormously popular in Russia.

One reason that the social system created by the Moscow ulus proved so stable and viable was that it solved life's biggest question. Centuries spent serving the tsar robbed generations of their spirit, their body and their willpower; in exchange, they received spiritual fulfilment and a reason to live. What the envoys who travelled to Moscow from the banks of the Rhine saw as despotism and slavery was regarded on the banks of the Moskva as selfless participation in a collective struggle. The tsar was both father and general, and the people were his children and soldiers. The absence of a private life was balanced by the prospect of dying a dulcet death for the good of your country, and the fatherland's expansion across space and time was a down payment for your salvation. Soul-saving is expensive.

The catastrophic blow that landed on the Moscow ulus did not come from its enemies on the battlefield, but from its own tsar – though it was unintentional. Europe was Russia's enemy number one, and the last thing on Peter the Great's mind was to 'Europeanise' his empire in the continent's hinterland. All the tsar actually wanted to do was modernise his army in preparation for war against the West, and to exploit the latest Western military technology. So he sent for guest workers. What came were people. And they brought words with them, words that disseminated hitherto unknown concepts such as 'freedom', 'republic', 'parliament', 'human rights' and 'personal dignity' throughout Russia.

From the start, Peter the Great's 'Europeanisation' of Russia was merely a case of misunderstanding on the part of the West. The reforming tsar had no intention of attuning the country to Western culture. Granted, he ordered people to wear foreign clothes, but that didn't change the fact that fear and violence remained the decisive forces of Russian life. It was therefore by no means part of his plan when the 'window to Europe' opened like a leak below the waterline. The system was now no longer insulated from ideas. And thus began the eighteenth-century incursion of liberal European values into Russia.

It didn't take long to see the results. Karl Peter Ulrich von Schleswig-Holstein-Gottorf – who, as Peter III, ruled Russia for a few months in 1762 before he was murdered by his wife, Catherine II – had just enough time to release the aristocracy from obligatory state service and allow them to freely travel abroad. It was a fateful blow. In the traditional Russian system, everyone, the country's entire population, was the tsar's – i.e. the state's – serf, and when the nobility was emancipated, the peasants who had once belonged to the tsar became the land-owners' slaves. Ironically, the first people to be freed in Russia themselves became slave owners. This partial liberation split a nation once 'united' in universal slavery.

From then on, the Russian soul was plagued by the question of how a free man could live in a country of slaves. The answer seemed obvious. The Russians started dreaming of upheavals that would break down the old structures, and of a democratic social order. The first attempt at a Russian revolution came with the so-called Decembrist Revolt in 1825, when officers who had received a European education exploited the period of confusion that arose when Alexander I died and his brother, Grand Duke Konstantin, renounced the throne in favour of their younger brother, Nicholas. The leaders of the revolt marched their soldiers to St Petersburg's Senate Square, and ordered them to demand a constitution (*konstitutsiya* in Russian). When a general (who, given that the soldiers could neither read nor write, wondered at their demands) asked, 'But what sort of *konstitutsiya* do you want, my brothers?' they replied: 'What do you mean, what kind? Our rightful tsar Konstantin's wife!' The revolt ended in bloodshed.

Through wars of conquest, Nicholas I and his predecessors had expanded the Moscow ulus into an enormous empire. Now the Russian tsars owned not only their own people, but countless other nations and tribes who spoke all sorts of languages and followed all sorts of religions. As before, this potpourri of nations was held together by fear and violence. Russia became a 'prison of nations'.

Yet the empire was gravely ill. It was suffering from dissociative identity disorder. A hundred years of unwanted education and enlightenment – to which Catherine the Great had also contributed, before turning away from her noble ideals, persecuting critics and tightening censorship – had played a nasty trick on a system that was no longer shielded from Western ideas. Because education goes hand in hand with the idea of individual freedom, Russia now witnessed the emergence of 'Russian Europeans', people who believed in Western values. The primacy of private life was a time bomb, ticking away under the bulky edifice that was Russia's totalitarian consciousness. Literature played a crucial role in all this. The first century of native Russian literature consisted chiefly of translations and imitations. There were no words to express the idea of human dignity. There was no verbal toolkit for the expression of individual consciousness; it had to be created first. And so the missing terms – the public sphere, being in love, humanity, literature – were introduced.

Over just a few generations, terms such as these created far-reaching socio-political change in Russia. They turned the country into a pair of conjoined twins who shared a body but whose heads were incapable of understanding each other. Ever since, Russia has been in the unique situation of having its territory shared by two spiritually and culturally disparate nations. Both are Russian, both speak the same language – but mentally they are opposites. One head is furnished with a European education, a love of freedom and the idea that Russia is part of a global human civilisation; it believes that the whole of Russian history is a bloody slough from which the country needs to be extricated, before being transformed into a liberal European society. This head refuses to live in a patriarchal dictatorship, and demands freedom, rights and a constitution. The other head has a traditional view of the world: it believes that the holy Rus is an island surrounded by a hostile ocean, and that only the father in the Kremlin and his iron fist can save this island and its people, and maintain order in Russia.

Pyotr Chaadayev, the first Russian philosopher, played a key role in the formation of the country's national consciousness. In the open letters he wrote between 1828 and 1830, he astonished Russia's emerging society with a simple idea: the Russians were not a people chosen by God. Russia, he argued, was outside history, Moscow was not the Third Rome, and, unlike the Messiah, the Russians had not been chosen to save the world – these notions were merely the result of a misunderstanding. 'The fatherland's misfortune,' he wrote, 'consists in our having adopted the Byzantine Orthodox faith, rather than the Roman Catholic faith; with this, we cut ourselves off from Europe and its evolution.' The idea, obvious as it was, exploded like a bomb in Russian brains. It was tantamount to mutiny. The monarch ordered that the author of the *Philosophical Letters* be declared insane. But his heretical writings appeared in the Samizdat of the time (*samizdat* means 'self-publishing', and the word was later used in the Communist Bloc to denote the unofficial channels that disseminated banned literature), and formed the basis for 'Westernism', one of the two main schools of Russian thought. While the ideology's adherents manned the barricades and declared war on the ulus, the 'Slavophiles' desperately sought to discover something in the continued existence of this prison of nations that could inspire hope.

Both sides felt uncomfortable in a system where the free and educated classes lived side by side with millions of serfs. Liberal social circles were appalled by slavery, but what worried the state was the prospect of a peasant revolt. In 1839, the chief of the secret police, Count Alexander von Benckendorff, told Tsar Nicholas I in a letter that 'serfdom is a powder keg under the state, and it is all the more dangerous because the army consists of these same peasants . . . It would be better to gradually, carefully start freeing them, than to wait until the process is started from below, by the people.' Nicholas tried to 'freeze' the country, but time was against him. His son Alexander II later introduced reforms that aimed to transform Russia into a 'European' country.

On 19 February 1861, exactly a hundred years after the nobility was freed, a decree was issued to abolish what remained of slavery, freeing the peasant serfs (as it turned out, only for a short time – for two generations or so; after the 1917 revolution, everyone was once again a slave of the state). Yet for the serfs, freedom came without property. All land remained in the hands of the squires. The peasants were disappointed and felt hoodwinked by the government, which led to uprisings. For the illiterate populace, freedom without land had little value.

The rest of the reforms introduced by Tsar Alexander sound like they were copied from democracy's pattern book: universal equality before the law, the separation of powers, an independent judiciary, the use of juries, public trials, the right to appeal and the right of the accused to independent counsel. He instituted a system of local government (*zemstvo*) involving provincial assemblies of elected delegates from every social class, and each city now had its own administrative body, such as the municipal dumas consisting of elected councillors. He granted autonomy to Russia's universities, introduced universal conscription and abolished corporal punishment. The country was moving towards a constitution in leaps and bounds. The ulus suffered one major defeat after another.

Not long after the emancipation of the serfs, however, journalists and authors began to foresee a new era of turmoil. To them, the democratisation of social life suggested that the iron fist that had hitherto protected the country from chaos was weakening.

The revolutionaries grew impatient and were eager to annihilate the despised tsarist regime. Because Alexander II, or 'Alexander the Liberator' as he was known, symbolised the existing system, he became the focus of their hatred. The educated classes, the intelligentsia, declared war on the government. 'Abolition of autocracy' and 'revolution' were the magic words that warmed the hearts and souls of well-read young men and women. They besieged the autocratic regime like a fortress, using Russian literature as a battering ram. Revolution became the flavour of the age. What bliss it would be to languish in prison before going to the gallows and crying out, with one's dying breath, 'Long live the revolution!' Until now, salvation had come from fighting for the tsar and his ulus. Now, the holy messianic war that Orthodox Russia had waged against its foes was replaced by an even holier and more messianic one – a war that would liberate the Russian people, and all mankind. The Russian soul, hungry for ideals, once again had a goal to which it could sacrifice its life: revolution.

The educated classes were wholeheartedly on the side of the revolutionaries, and supported them in their war against the tsarist regime by any means possible. The intelligentsia was sympathetic to terrorists too, as evidenced by the famous 1878 case of the terrorist Vera Zasulich, whose acquittal of attempting to assassinate a tsarist official was met with great cheers.

After several assassination attempts, Alexander II was finally killed by a bomb on 1 March 1881, the very same day he signed the decree that would have marked the country's first step towards a constitution. Under his successor, the 'great reforms' were put on hold. It was the progressive forces, therefore, who stymied reform, because they thought the changes being made to the tsarist system didn't go far enough.

A drama for three actors was being staged in Russia: the people were silent (as Pushkin so brilliantly puts it in the last line of his verse tragedy *Boris Godunov*), while the educated classes demanded direct democracy and declared war on the government; all that the third actor, the state, could do was either retreat further and further until its humiliating defeat, or tighten the screws. The new tsar, Alexander III, placed Russia into a brief ice age. His son Nicholas II decided to retreat.

Fate was ill-disposed towards the last pre-Soviet tsar. He lost the war with Japan, and immediately faced revolution in his own country. In Russia, a regime's lifespan has always been lengthened by military victories and shortened by defeat. Every time a ruler has retreated, society has demanded further concessions. In 1905, Russia introduced political freedoms, a constitution cementing the principle of separation of powers, and a parliament, the Duma. To go further would have required nothing short of the dissolution of the monarchy and the proclamation of a republic – and this is what happened soon after, in February 1917. Those who had laid down their lives for the revolution in the preceding decades were luckier than those who survived long enough to see its triumph. Looking back on the twentieth century, the 'bloodthirsty tyrant' Nicholas II turns out to have been a quiet, harmless martyr of the revolution.

The February Revolution of 1917 certified Russia as the most democratic country in the world: all class privilege was erased, universal freedom of religion and thought were guaranteed, and – earlier than in many Western states – women were given the vote. The prison of nations broke up, and its people dispersed the moment they realised that the padlock was open and the guards had gone off to a revolutionary rally. The newly founded states rushed to declare their independence from Russia.

Russian society had finally defeated the empire's government. The iron fist had long grown rusty, and crumbled. The people would have continued to stay silent, but then, as predicted, chaos broke out. What happened then was the worst that can happen to an ulus: the top-down power structure imploded, even as the country was still at war, and suddenly millions of armed men who had been torn from their homes were practically left to their own devices, without any superiors to issue orders – starving, embittered by defeat, furious, and incited against their wealthier fellow citizens. The world war broke the neck of the newborn Russian democracy.

The revolutionary parties' slogans, such as 'Steal what has been stolen from you!', resonated far more with the Russian peasants than the moderate provisional government's warning against overly radical demands and extreme actions. All over the country, estates were set on fire. Libraries and other cultural assets were among the first victims. Street crime proliferated. The entire infrastructure collapsed. The country was overwhelmed by an anarchy so bloody that it took an even bloodier dictatorship to restore order. The provisional democratic government simply had not had enough time to implement new political institutions. It hadn't even been able to usher in a people's assembly.

What was needed was a modern equivalent to the iron fist. The Moscow ulus's incarnation as a tsarist monarchy was outdated, and couldn't possibly be reanimated. Yet history always offers a choice of avatars, and it didn't take long to find a replacement. Lenin, Trotsky and the other communist leaders were the fanatical followers of a false Western doctrine, and history wasted no time in using them to resurrect the Moscow ulus. They thought they had been chosen to change the course of history – this was their romantic motive in the bitter fight for power – but the methods by which they seized power and their concept of dictatorship coincided neatly with the ideas and methods of the Great Khans. Marxist rhetoric provided the perfect camouflage. The Bolsheviks thought they were saving the world from capitalism, but were in fact merely used to salvage the Russian empire.

The most liberal of all social orders took just a few months to destroy the country, before being replaced by the least liberal. The rebuilding of the ulus happened quickly. There was no need to reinvent the wheel – the past had all the necessary actions and tools at the ready. The new regime created the secret police, the killing machine known as the Cheka (which later became the GPU, NKVD, KGB and FSB), just three weeks after seizing power. The Party transformed into a proxy Church, and the messianic mission of the re-established empire was now 'socialist' rather than religious. The Third International rhymed perfectly with the Third Rome.

The time of the great multinational empires was apparently over – the Austro-Hungarian and Ottoman empires had gone under, and the Russian empire should by rights also have disappeared from the face of the earth. But the Moscow ulus was a fundamentally different kind of empire. History had an ace up its sleeve: the Bolsheviks who were now in charge would 'free' not only the Russians, but all nations. The people and territories that had uncoupled from Moscow and declared their independence (Ukraine, the republics of the Caucasus, Central Asia and the far east) were regained in Russia's 'civil' war. A civil war is an armed conflict between different groups inside the borders of one state; describing the conquest of those independent countries as a 'civil war' was a Soviet propaganda trick.

The process of restoring order to the country was sharply reminiscent of the Mongols' brutality under Nevsky. They may not have ripped out tongues and gouged out eyes, but the relationship between those in power and the people was again firmly grounded in sheer terror. The Bolsheviks reinforced their dictatorship by shooting hostages randomly picked from among the affluent and educated. The exploiting classes had to be exterminated. In other words, the intelligentsia was erased. This genocide based on class followed a historical logic: when the Moscow ulus split into two nations and a spiritually 'European' Russia emerged, the system collapsed; hence the head of the westwards-gazing conjoined twin had to be chopped off. Which is exactly what they did.

The eradication of the 'exploiters' was only the beginning. The terror slowly ground its way through the entire country and every social class. Ultimately, though, the 'exploited classes' were again the victims, as millions of peasants were executed or starved to death. The deployment of naked violence hid behind the moral mask of 'class war'. The Bolsheviks succeeded in turning the people into their own executioners.

The ulus was hitting back. Peter the Great had once opened the 'window to Europe'; Stalin tightly locked it, isolating the country anew from the outside world. The communist romantics were made to step aside (usually with a shot in the back of the neck) to clear the way for the creation of an Asian despotism whose relationship to a Marxist utopia was exposed as only so much ideological chatter, such as its assertion of 'the right of nations to self-determination'. There was only one slogan of Marx's that real socialism took seriously: 'Violence is the midwife of history.'

The Moscow ulus was resurrected in all its glory. The 'one true faith' was recoded from Orthodoxy to communism, but that didn't affect the mythological consciousness of its millions of citizens. Again, a military empire was treating its own people as soldiers. An autocrat was idolised by his subjects. The whole nation cheered in unison when traitors were executed. The lowly masses and higher ranks were united in slavery. The sole aim was victory over the enemy. 'We will take the fight to the aggressor!' The point of a Russian's life was to serve the Soviet Union. Dying for their fatherland was supreme bliss. The mere suggestion of personal initiative, the mere flicker of a free thought, amounted to a 'Trotskyist conspiracy'. Any expression of discontent, no matter how justified, was an 'act of sabotage'. There was no private ownership: the state owned everything – and everyone. There was also only one god – the living god who sat in the Kremlin. The Great Khan flaunted his omnipotence and allowed his subjects to kiss his feet. Stalin created the perfect personal dictatorship, and not a single attempt was made on the life of the 'father of the workers of the world'. Like Dracula before him, Stalin was feared and loved by his people.

The war was evidence of the modernised ulus's resilience. When the dictator thought that he might lose his power and his life, he turned to the people, calling them his 'brothers and sisters' – and the slaves gave their lives 'for the fatherland! For Stalin!' Homeland and dictator: two for the price of one.

The state had passed a tough test, which had claimed countless victims. They perfected the system. Stalin officially abandoned internationalism, the ideological basis for the Marxist super-stition. He resurrected the Orthodox Church, patriotism and national heroes like Prince Alexander Nevsky and Field Marshal Suvorov (one of the greatest military strategists of the eighteenth century) from the ashes of the revolution. 'Stalin Raised Us' replaced the workers' song, 'The Internationale', as the national anthem.

No enemy, no matter who they are, stands a chance in a war against such a system. When a military strategy consists of tirelessly burning through thousands upon thousands of soldiers, the winner will always be the general who doesn't spare a single life and has an inexhaustible supply of reserves at their disposal. As the 'Marshal of Victory', Georgy Zhukov, head of the Red Army and Soviet minister of defence in the 1950s, put it bluntly: 'No matter. Russian women will give birth to more.'

To this day, historians disagree about how many people died in the war, how many victims the purges claimed, how many people were arrested, shot dead or starved to death. They will probably go on disagreeing for a long time. They may even never be able to determine the real number.

Dmitri Mendeleev, the famous chemist and creator of the periodic table, was also interested in sociology and demographics. At the end of the nineteenth century, he looked at Russia's economic growth figures and current birth rate, and forecast that in 1950 the empire would comprise between 450 and 500 million people. But Mendeleev hadn't accounted for the future genocide of the people by their own government. In 1950, the official population figure for the new Russian empire was 179 million. 'No matter. Russian women will give birth to more.'

After its victory over Germany, the prison of nations was expanded to accommodate a new cohort of Eastern European inmates. These 'socialist brothers' now all had to learn Russian, the occupier's language. The language of Pushkin and Tolstoy. They had to learn to distinguish Russian culture from Russian tyranny. Not necessarily an easy task.

In the British empire, the British enjoyed special privileges. The Russian empire, however, was not the Russians' empire. The eponymous people were the most oppressed and exploited in the whole 'socialist camp'. They lived in the worst conditions, and it was from them that the Soviet Union exacted the most victims and the heaviest sacrifices. So whose empire was it?

The Russian ulus exists not for the benefit of the Russians, but for those who run it. Holding on to power was and remains the ulus's one and only ideology.

Chapter 3

Скоро! – Soon!

I was born the year of the first human space flight. To this day, the Russians are proud of Gagarin. That same year, Stalin was moved out of the mausoleum in Red Square in a covert operation, and the Party Congress approved a new plan: in twenty years – in the brightly shining, far-away year of 1980 – the Soviet people would be living under communism.

It was still the time of the 'Great Thaw'. Following Stalin's death, the Gulag shrank, those who had been executed were posthumously declared innocent and rehabilitated, and it looked like the regime's iron fist was loosening its chokehold. But those who wielded that fist didn't really mean it. In 1956, they brutally crushed the people's revolt in Hungary. In 1962, Soviet troops opened fire on a workers' protest in Novocherkassk, and seven of the strike's supposed ringleaders were subsequently tried and executed.

The year I was born was also the year that the Berlin Wall went up. The Moscow ulus was marking its territory. My first 'political' memory is of being three years old; it was dark outside and raining, and I wanted to stay indoors and play. Instead, they dragged me out into the wet and cold to queue outside our grocer's. You could buy flour there that day, but because each person was only allowed to buy a certain amount, every child counted. Much later, I was able to link this childhood memory to a political event: in autumn 1964, artificial bottle-necks created as part of the plot to remove Khrushchev resulted in a shortage of basic foodstuffs, which then all of a sudden reappeared in the shops after he was ousted.

Soviet children were supposed to be the happiest children on the planet. And I actually was. After all, children are immune to the shenanigans of grown-ups. Nurseries and schools were saturated with Lenin, but communist ideology had long ago lost its halo, and the things we were taught to hold sacred merely served as the butt of our jokes. All that really remained sacred was people's memory of the war. The 9th of May was their Day of Truth.

These were the days of the Cold War, but that war was happening somewhere far away. It came to us as news reports we didn't watch, and in sports broadcasts. For us, even the fight for the puck symbolised the war between the two systems. Oh, how we looked forward to beating the Americans and Canadians in the Olympics! The ice hockey battles we fought against Czechoslovakia were especially tough. It was their revenge for

1968. 'You beat us with tanks, we beat you with goals,' went our opponents' slogan. We naturally rooted passionately for our team during those acrimonious battles against our 'brother republic'. Those ungrateful Czechs – we liberated them from German fascism, and they repay us with hate!

Young children don't notice the utter mendacity of the world around them; but as they get older, they find it distressing and demeaning. My self-awareness was awakened in senior school – and it was a painful experience.

The fossilised propagandists operated as if on autopilot, conning the population with fairy tales of the Soviet order's achievements and parading tanks and rockets in Red Square by way of proof, while the Soviet people, the 'proud builders of communism', spent their days searching for scarce goods and wiping their arses with scraps torn from *Pravda* which declared that we lived in the best of all possible worlds.

The false doctrine was rotting, and it stank. The state didn't dare to consign it to the dustbin of history just yet. They taught Marxist dogma in the schools, but it was furtively ridiculed even in the staffroom. In accordance with the law of inertia, they paid homage to the revolution of 1917, but it was clear to everyone that all those victims sacrificed to the Bolsheviks' ideals had been sacrificed for no reason. Millions of people had been murdered in vain.

The borders may have been sealed, but the latest technology started pricking holes in the Iron Curtain. We were able to receive Western radio stations, if not without interference. Yet the Soviet people themselves were even more effective contributors to 'enemy' propaganda: diplomats, journalists and athletes brought back clothes, gadgets and records from the West. Jeans were the propaganda war's greatest coup. The successful defections of famous musicians, artists, dancers and diplomats gave Soviet brains much food for thought.

Slowly but surely, the conjoined brother's severed head started to grow back. The censors tried to excise all signs of life, but they were fighting a losing battle. The increasing availability of typewriters inevitably ushered in the Samizdat. As soon as there were tape recorders, songs by Bulat Okudzhava, Alexander Galich and Vladimir Vysotsky became famous all over the country.

In this suffocating and demeaning atmosphere, many Russians found in literature the key to their survival. I was one of them. It was my brother Sasha, who opened my eyes to this life-saving world. He was six years older than me, and belonged to a network of people who shared books. I would sit in a corner of the room and listen as his friends talked about banned poets. Even just this, being able to speak freely, meant a lot. By doing nothing more than reading and talking, you were already engaged in the fight. A little one-man war to preserve your dignity in this mendacious world.

When I was sixteen, I dreamt of two things: becoming a writer and travelling the world. Realising that my parents had been slaves all their lives, and had brought me into this prison world as a slave, was my childhood trauma. I felt betrayed. I knew now that my country was separated from the rest of the world by barbed wire. The books I wanted to write wouldn't conform to the rules of the regime, which meant that they would not be published; and travelling abroad was forbidden anyhow. We were only allowed to travel as far as the limits of our habitat. This was something, at least, and we did enjoy doing that. The experiences we made along the way enriched our understanding of our home country. We learnt something new every time. I'll never forget the journey my first girlfriend and I – both eighteen at the time – went on around our 'western Europe', that is, the Baltic states. We did have many wonderful encounters, though some of them left wounds too. In Tallinn, the first city we visited, we once asked for directions – in Russian, obviously – but received no response. In a way, the response was clear: we were the occupier, and you didn't talk to the occupier. How could I explain to these people that I wasn't an occupier? That we wanted 'your and our freedom'? That we had a common enemy, that this occupying power had taken over my city too?

I learnt an important lesson then: I was responsible for everything – for my language, my home country, my history, my parents and grandparents, the ancestors I never knew, everything that my people did or didn't do. For everything.

It was painful, but now I am grateful to the people in Tallinn who walked past us without a word.

Yes, I was the occupier, I was a slave belonging to the occupying power. I didn't even own my own body. At school, they taught us to march and how to take a Kalashnikov apart and put it back together again, blindfolded. They were already preparing us for the next war. The next one, though we didn't know it yet, would take place in Afghanistan. The only thing that was mine were my thoughts and the things I read. They couldn't take that away from me, or at least only by taking my head. Reading was the only possible form of defence. All you had to do was read a banned author, for example Nabokov, to feel like you were manning the barricades. It sounds paradoxical these days, but Nabokov symbolised our fight. Here in the West, he was a bestselling author who toyed with his readers' sex drive, but in Russia his books were read as a rousing protest against the regime. We mainly read his Russian novels, in which there was nothing political, but for Nabokov the apolitical was itself a weapon against the totalitarian system. He was banned in the Soviet Union, despite the fact that he didn't openly criticise it in his writings. The Soviet Union had nuclear missiles, but was afraid of authors like the man who wrote *Lolita* – let alone authors like Shalamov and Solzhenitsyn.

Books such as *To Build a Castle* by Vladimir Bukovsky or *To Be Preserved Forever* and *The Education of a True Believer* by Lev Kopelev reorientated my adolescent consciousness. Reading these books gave me hope and strength, the air to breathe and the courage to live.

The Berlin Wall visibly marked the border – but only for the West. When I was young, the border was invisible. It didn't run through the country, but through each of us. You yourself determined where your freedom ended. The barbed wire was invisible, but we all knew where it was. Your survival instinct would set off a warning siren whenever you got too close to it. Dissidents, however, walked into it deliberately.

These people practically fought the system single-handedly, without any prospect of victory. No one in the whole of that vast country ever heard about their protest actions. Their lives were destroyed, and they endured years in prison or psychiatric hospitals. And yet they didn't give up. I can still clearly remember my mother and brother having heated discussions about it. She was scared that he would end up in prison, which he did. (My father thought dissidents were traitors, not heroes – end of discussion.) She thought their sacrifice pointless, and that it was immoral to use lofty words to entice young people into ruining their lives. You couldn't blame her for being scared. It was her survivor's wisdom.

My mother didn't understand that these people weren't victims. They consciously chose freedom, every time. Whenever they were given an opportunity to renounce the fight, they always decided for themselves, even if it meant choosing prison or death. They were the only truly free people in this prison state. And freedom came at a high price.

The distant star of 1980 drew nearer. No one mentioned the Party's promise of communism; but then, they no longer cared, neither the higher ranks nor the 'lowly masses'. Everyone knew that the whole system was in decay. The Soviet Union was a rotten state, rattling its nuclear weapons despite being incapable of providing its wretched people with food or other basic necessities. This was nothing new – it had been like this in Stalin's day. The difference was that our Great Khan was now old and frail and no one was afraid of him any more. Under Brezhnev, the screws loosened; the 'vertical of power' was allowed to act with utter impunity, and the country became immersed in corruption, double-dealing and out-and-out thievery.

One of the key reasons why the Soviet empire lost the Cold War was that the West had a cunning new weapon in its arsenal: VCRs. We had more than enough tanks, but there was no way to protect ourselves against those videotapes infected with the Hollywood virus. The plots of the films we saw may not have been particularly exciting, but the clothes, furniture, food and cars dazzled us starving, impoverished Soviet people. We'd had enough of the lies, the slogans and promises of a bright future. We wanted to live today. That dried-out system, which subsisted on nothing but war, was decomposing from the inside out and dragging itself towards its end.

In 1979, the Afghan War began. No one wanted it, not even the senile old men in the Politburo, but the ulus forced them to rule according to its law. Empires live off wars. Victories prolong their existence, but each defeat brings them a step closer to collapse: whereas Stalin's triumph in the Second World War only empowered the Gulag state, the Afghan disaster accelerated the end of the USSR.

Coffins started arriving from Afghanistan. Family members were prohibited from marking the place of death on the gravestones: I remember our Aunt Lida, Mum's cousin from Zaporizhzhia, taking a folded handkerchief out of her handbag, laying it on the table and carefully opening it. Inside was a piece of Afghan soil, taken from the place where her son was killed. His friend, who had served with him in Afghanistan, had brought it back for her. A little piece of dried-up mud. Nothing special. She carefully wrapped it up again, pressed it to her breast and began to cry.

I was a student at the teaching institute at the time, which had a military faculty. This meant that I would not be going to Afghanistan. We were being trained as military interpreters, and learnt how to translate interrogations of West German POWs – just in case there was another war with Germany.

The following year, instead of the promised advent of communism, we got the Moscow Olympics. The occupying power that had taken its own people hostage expected democratic governments to signal their acceptance of Russian aggression in Afghanistan by taking part in the Olympics. But it didn't turn out that way. The democratic countries wanted to show that they stood in solidarity with the hostages, not with the hostage-takers, and boycotted the games. The satellite states were practically the only ones who came. Switzerland also sent a team, its more than seventy athletes competing under the neutral Olympic flag. Were the two medals they won (in the absence of the best athletes in the world) worth this show of solidarity with the Russian government?

At the institute, they trained us as city guides for the West

German tourists who would be coming for the Games. I remember a 'civilian' teacher coaching us in how to correctly answer potentially provocative questions from Westerners. 'Why can't you buy anything in the shops for locals, but get whatever you want for hard cash in special shops for foreigners?' he asked. A long silence ensued. You could have heard a pin drop. Asking such questions in public usually brought with it unpleasant consequences. He then gave us the correct answer: 'To be honest, yes, there are shortages. But when we have guests, we offer them the very best, even if it's something we can't afford ourselves.' Our training proved a waste of time: the Western guests stayed away, and the groups of tourists from East Germany we looked after didn't ask such questions.

After Brezhnev came Yuri Andropov, the head of the KGB. For a while it seemed as if the screws would tighten once again. Our fear grew.

One day, a form at the school where my mother was head organised a 'Vysotsky evening' – in memory of the Russian singer who had fallen out of favour with the state, and who had died two years earlier. My mother had given them permission to do it. It was a fateful decision. Immediately after the musical evening, some of the parents reported her to the regional education authority. She was sacked, and had to leave the school where she had worked for thirty years, first as a teacher, then as head. The school was her life, and when she couldn't work any more she fell ill. It was cancer. She was admitted to several different hospitals and had multiple operations. The disease tortured her for years.

At the same time, on top of everything else, my brother was sent to prison. Under Andropov, things that had once been tolerated – books, videos, conversations – got you arrested. I visited my brother in the prison camp, first in Lgov near Kursk, later in Ivdel in the Northern Urals. These journeys, too, broadened my image of Russia.

It looked as if the system would continue to vegetate away for decades, if not centuries. Then came 1984. Countries don't believe their own prophets. In the late 1960s, Andrei Amalrik, a well-known dissident, wrote a famous book called *Will the Soviet Union Survive until 1984?*, in which he argued that the Soviet Union would have collapsed by then. Who in the 1960s expected that Amalrik would be proved right – if out by a few years?

Then a miracle happened. The senile old men in the Kremlin died one after the other, and an ambitious young party secretary from Krasnodar took the helm. Suddenly, the magical word 'perestroika' came along and changed our lives. Hope returned to the country. In truth, Gorbachev wanted modernisation only because he thought it necessary to save the regime. He by no means wanted Russia to become an actual democracy, or to have free elections without the Party. But his slogans took on a life of their own.

The dissidents appeared to have won the fight and defeated the regime after all. They started printing previously banned books, and all of a sudden you could say what you really thought. Freedom also arrived literally: my brother was released and returned from Ivdel in time to see his mother before she died.

My mother was in agony. She wanted to die, but she couldn't – not until Sasha came home. A few months before her death, she started losing her voice. She was in severe pain, and whispered that she had no strength left. She only wanted to wait for Sasha. She listened to the radio all the time. When I visited her in hospital, I told her that we were organising protest rallies against the Party. I was excited and hopeful; she feared that things would end badly.

For some, perestroika above all meant turning the system into a democracy, for others it meant the lack of a firm hand, impending chaos and anarchy. The conquered nations saw it as a chance to be released from their prison. On the edges of the empire, blood had already started flowing.

One day, I was sitting at my mother's bedside in a hospital in Sokolniki after she had undergone an operation. She lay there for a long time with her eyes closed. Then she opened them and said, 'Who'd have thought it!' 'What?' I asked her. 'How everything repeats itself. This is the same hospital in Sokolniki where we brought my mother. She was on a different ward, though. She died here, in fifty-three. Back then, the news was full of the Kremlin Doctors' Plot. And now there's this perestroika.'

The radio stations were broadcasting news bulletins from

Tbilisi, where tens of thousands of demonstrators had gathered outside the government building on Rustaveli Avenue, calling for Georgia to exit the Soviet Union. The night the protest was crushed, they reported armoured tanks rolling over people, and soldiers killing demonstrators with field shovels.

My mother died a few days after my brother came home from prison. I'm convinced that even if Sasha had stayed in prison for several more months, she would have held out for his return.

When perestroika started, I began teaching at a school. A new life, I thought, could and had to start with the children, with school. When Soviet power crumbled, I experienced the unfamiliar, wonderful feeling of being a citizen of my country whose future was in his own hands. It was the first time I felt that I could make a difference. I wanted to make my country a better place. Suddenly, I was in the right place at the right time. I believed that the days of prison rules, the days of 'the strongest gets the best bunk', were finally over. A new life was beginning, a life based on the most important law of all: the preservation of human dignity.

Schools mirror the social order in which they exist; and so did the Russian schools: when an iron fist is in charge, order reigns. At school, I sensed that I was swimming against the tide, against teachers, parents and children. I was so confident, so convinced by my point of view. I felt so strong that I didn't doubt for a moment I'd be able to pull them all along with me. The events that were happening in the country gave me even more strength and confidence. I thought I was changing the country. Before my very eyes, totalitarian Russia was transforming into a democratic state. It was a fantastic moment.

The further democracy progressed in Russia, the harder it was to get your hands on necessities. Everything was in short supply. The food rations my father received as a war veteran included donations from West Germany. In my father's eyes, the collapse of the Soviet Union represented a defeat in the same war he had fought in as a young man, together with the rest of the country. My father hated Gorbachev. I didn't like Gorbachev either, but for a different reason – because he was doing everything in his power to stop the USSR and the Soviet system from collapsing. As history unfolded before our eyes, my father and I looked on from opposite banks of the river.

Russia was staging the same drama for three actors it had staged a hundred years earlier. The state did all it could – including launching military operations in Lithuania and Georgia – to get the genie of freedom back into the bottle. The people were confused, and worked hard to survive the approaching chaos. 'Every man for himself' was the slogan of the day. The freshly roused civil society protested in Moscow's city centre, demanding 'European' freedoms and the complete dismantling of the much-hated one-party system. My friends and I attended every single rally, right from the start. We firmly believed that we'd win. It was all so plain and simple: a gang of communists had taken over our country, and if we sent the Party to the devil, the borders would open and we'd return once again to the global family of nations – who live according to the laws of democracy, freedom and commitment to the rights of the individual.

Visas were the symbol of the new freedom, a tangible consequence of the fall of the Iron Curtain. Neither my father nor my mother had ever crossed a border. My father would joke, 'I'm just like Pushkin.' It was a comforting thought for him. Pushkin was forbidden from leaving the country and spent his whole life in Russia, yet this had by no means stopped him from becoming the pride of the nation.

When the Iron Curtain had rusted through and I went abroad for the first time, I wasn't merely a tourist. The unspeakable freedom I felt was that of someone who has just been released from prison. He stands in the street in a city somewhere, breathing. And in that instant, the simple street is more than a street. Much more.

The first time I went to the West was in 1989, before the Wall came down. I clearly remember how wonderful it was to cross the border. I was only able to put it into words later, when I discovered these words by Nikolai Karamzin, in *Letters of a Russian Traveller*: 'It seems as if the local air has something revivifying about it. I can breathe more easily and more freely, my step is surer, I hold my head higher, and I proudly remember that I am human.' He wrote this in 1789, exactly two hundred years earlier.

Back in September 1989, I spent a week in East Berlin, staying with friends. Every day, I would walk through the Wall to the

Western side – because I came from a country where perestroika was the order of the day, and there was a West German visa in my passport. My friends in East Berlin were surprised, envious of me and angry, because they weren't allowed to cross. I tried to convince them that, soon, they would be free too. They didn't believe me. I still remember looking at the Western side of the Wall: there were no guards to be seen. Anyone who fancied it left behind a piece of graffiti. I borrowed a spray can from some youths, and wrote '*СКОРО!*' on it, Russian for 'soon'. I still have a photo of me spraying those letters onto the wall in green paint. Even if no one noticed them, it was important to me to write this word. It was my personal dialogue with world history. In those days, I didn't yet have a single grey hair. I was young and happy, if not particularly aware of it.

The occupying power retreated – up to a point. Then it stood there, with its back to the abyss. The Party's *nomenklatura* hit back, and in August 1991 its top echelons made a last-ditch attempt to hold on to power.

In the early hours of 19 August, the State Committee on the State of Emergency announced on Moscow TV that President Mikhail Gorbachev was unwell, and that it was thus forced to take charge of the situation in the country. The junta declared a state of emergency, and sent tanks into Moscow's streets. On TV, they showed Pyotr Tchaikovsky's *Swan Lake* on an endless loop – it sounded like a funeral march. The coup was under way.

I remember that day well. It was the summer holidays. There

was a light rain. My wife was in our dacha near Moscow with our three-year-old son. I walked through the streets in the centre of Moscow, which were barricaded by armoured tanks. Never before in my life had I felt this bad. I felt like someone who has escaped prison and thinks he's free, only to be recaptured. I simply didn't want to carry on living. I think many of my fellow Russians felt the same way.

Towards evening, I took a suburban train to Zagoryansky. The trains are normally noisy, with people talking, telling stories, laughing, arguing. This time, everyone was just sitting there quietly. What would come next – a dictatorship? Would fear and lies reign once again? It was heart-breaking. Suddenly, someone walked in from another carriage and said, 'People! Fellow citizens! The communist bandits want to get back in power. But we won't allow it. We won't give in to them. Come to the White House! They've already set up barricades there!' For a moment, all was silent. Then someone started clapping. Then the whole carriage clapped. Some had tears in their eyes.

The next day, I went to the White House on the banks of the Moskva. The White House was the seat of the democratically elected government, which had declared that the State Committee was plotting its overthrow. I remember the faces of the people on the barricades. People who are prepared to fight for their freedom have beautiful faces. I suddenly spotted boys from my form among them. They had come too – I can't describe how happy that made me. Maybe I wasn't all that bad at my job.

Back then, we won. Those were happy days. What else can you be, when you're standing outside the notorious KGB building on Lubyanka Square, watching them topple the statue of Dzerzhinsky, the Soviet Union's executioner-in-chief? The next day, I was among the cheering crowd outside the Central Committee building as they tore the red flag from the facade of the Party headquarters. The Party was finished! It was a historic moment. There were lots of foreign TV crews there; right behind me, Gerd Ruge from West German TV was trying to interview members of the crowd. I was very excited, but still managed to say a few words in German. I told him how I felt at that moment, and finished by saying, 'I'm glad to know that my son, who's three now, will be growing up in a free, democratic Russia.'

Chapter 4

The New Era of Turmoil

In August 1991, three young people died defending the White House. We went to their funeral. Countless people attended.

That a military coup which could have cost thousands of lives ended without more bloodshed seemed symbolic. We wanted to believe that Russia had swallowed its fill of the twentieth-century's bloody gruel, and that this would be the beginning of a life lived according to new laws, laws that guaranteed our human dignity. Crucially, there must be no more bloodshed. That the three dead were an Orthodox Christian, a Muslim and a Jew also seemed auspicious. They had sacrificed their lives for our common fatherland – for a new, free Russia. We thought that theirs would be the last drop of blood to flow in our country.

Unfortunately, it was only the first blood drawn by the new

Russia. The Age of Hope was nearing its end. The Age of Disappointment dawned.

Our hopes centred on the country's rapid transformation into a democracy, a market economy and a civil society orientated on Western ideas. We knew that it wouldn't be a walk in the park, but the way in which the new democratic order was introduced did make us wonder.

In the Soviet Union, every asset in the country belonged to the Soviet people – at least, that was what the government solemnly declared. In reality, everything belonged to the state, meaning that it belonged to no one. Now, though, all state property would be privatised in a fair and transparent process, and then truly belong to the people. A democratic society could not be built on the dispossessed; to create a 'European' social order, you needed high levels of private ownership. So the new leadership decided that every citizen, young and old, would receive a voucher with a nominal value of 10,000 roubles, which they could exchange for shares in Russian companies.

A government TV advert assured viewers that each voucher was worth two Volga cars. I can still clearly recall how my family and I worked out which companies to acquire shares in when we received those promising vouchers in the summer of 1992.

Shady characters started turning up at our local metro station to buy up people's vouchers. The strange thing was that those bits of paper that were supposedly worth two Volgas were going for less than their nominal value. The price dropped every day, faster and faster, and eventually a voucher was worth just two bottles of vodka. Only those who sold theirs right away gained anything. It quickly dawned on us that our family, like millions of others, had been shamefully conned by the new democratic government. Meanwhile, the 'red directors' (i.e. Soviet business leaders) and former party and Komsomol functionaries were rushing to privatise every imaginable and unimaginable state asset. Voucher privatisation left the overwhelming majority of people empty-handed. This massive country's assets, including natural resources, passed wholesale into the hands of a few of the old communist elite, who rose from the ashes of their political past by mutating into capitalists. Most people were only admitted as spectators to this privatisation process, whose battle cry was 'Grab what you can'.

Anatoly Chubais, the spiritual father of voucher privatisation, later justified his actions by claiming that 'we did not have a choice between an "honest" privatisation and a "dishonest" one, because an honest privatisation means clear rules imposed by a strong state that can enforce its laws. In the early 1990s, we had no state and no law enforcement . . . Our choice was between bandit communism or bandit capitalism.'*

It didn't take long for the democratic revolution to be sold down the river. It is evidently an immutable law of all revolutions that they be led by people who are prepared to sacrifice their lives for their country's freedom and for human dignity;

---

* Arkady Ostrovsky, 'Dinner with the FT: Father to the Oligarchs', *Financial Times*, 23 November 2004, <https://www.ft.com/content/763b10fc-337e-11d9-b6c3-00000e2511c8>.

but then the best of them die in battle, and afterwards it's the cynics and profiteers who rise to power, and life returns to its never-ending, unchanging groove. The majority of Russia's inhabitants couldn't enjoy the freedom of the press, open borders and other democratic achievements. What they desperately needed was jobs, an income. The decrepit economy was on its last legs, hyperinflation was devouring everyone's pay cheque and pensions melted away. Many found that the savings they had accumulated during the development of the socialist state had gone down the drain. Nothing was certain any more, neither the past nor the future. Everything was in chaos. For millions and millions of people, life became purely a question of survival. Blood flowed in Russian streets as criminal gangs fought interminable battles. But all the government could do was promise the battered people 'shock therapy'.

In 1991, they cheered 'Yeltsin! Yeltsin!' Now, two years later, they were chanting 'Lock Yeltsin and his cronies up!' at mass rallies.

A feud developed between the new democratic president and the Supreme Soviet, which had been elected when the Soviet Union was still in existence. Yeltsin backed the 'shock therapy' advocated by economic reformers working under Yegor Gaidar. The deputies, however, blocked the reforms and resisted predatory privatisation. An acrimonious power struggle ensued. In autumn 1993, things came to a head. On 21 September, Yeltsin signed Ukaz 1400, a decree announcing the summary dissolution of parliament – although he didn't officially have the power to do so. The constitutional court declared the *ukaz* unconstitutional. Parliament held a vote and decided to depose Yeltsin, and appointed his former comrade-in-arms and vice president General Alexander Rutskoy as the new president. Now, Russia had two presidents.

The deputies of the Supreme Soviet condemned Yeltsin's *ukaz* as a coup d'état. They continued to meet in the White House, and called on the people to rise up against the 'putschist', Yeltsin. When the electricity supply to the White House was switched off, they armed themselves and barricaded themselves inside the building, meeting by candlelight.

Again, barricades surrounded the White House. This time, though, they were manned by very different people. It was a diverse group, but most were nationalist communists led by the anti-Semite Albert Makashov. During those mass rallies against the Communist Party, we had chanted, 'We are the people!' But these people were also 'the people'. They were the other Russian people. This was a popular uprising against unfettered and unfair privatisation, against 'shock therapy', against poverty and anarchy. Now, it was this other Russian people marching through the streets, and against whom the tanks were defending us. Confusion and resentment were everywhere.

The siege lasted several days. I, too, visited the square in front of the White House. There were lots of red banners, but also people waving the tsarist monarchy's black, yellow and white flag (the nationalists weren't happy with the break-up of the Soviet Union, and wanted the separatist states back). People were sitting around bonfires singing old Soviet songs, their faces grim and determined, their skin and clothes black from the smoke. There were many women among them, including older ones, who had lived through the war. Around one bonfire, they were singing 'Arise, Great Country!' It's the most famous Soviet-era war song, officially called 'The Sacred War'. These men and women from among the poorest sections of society saw the democrats as fascists and agents of the US occupying their fatherland, and wanted to liberate their country. Later, the police cordoned off the entire sector around the White House, and you couldn't get through any more.

The tension rose day by day. The country was paralysed by this confrontation between the two centres of power. Something had to give. Suddenly, the tension exploded in violence, a vicious fight to the death. A lot of blood flowed. This was not how I'd pictured Russia's democratic future.

I remember that 3rd of October well. It was a Sunday, and I'd been for a walk with my son, down to the Yauza river and past the stadium. It was a glorious, almost summery day. Back home, my son sat down in front of the TV to watch *Teenage Mutant Ninja Turtles*. We were in the kitchen. All of a sudden, he came running in, sobbing. His programme had been interrupted by a special news bulletin: the communists were descending on the TV centre in Ostankino. Somehow, I managed to calm him down. I sat him at the table and gave him some colouring pencils to draw with. We turned on the radio and listened to the news. A crowd had broken through the outer ring of the barricades around the White House, and thousands were streaming into Ostankino to support the Supreme Soviet. They had already stormed the tall municipal government building, and now there was fighting around the TV centre. A little later, I checked on my son. He was deeply engrossed in his drawing, his tongue between his teeth, and muttering to himself as he moved the pencil across the sheet with such force that the tip broke off. I asked him what he was drawing. 'The Ninja Turtles,' he replied. 'They're hitting the communists.' He was defending his world with colouring pencils.

The assault on the TV centre was unsuccessful. Soldiers shot into the crowd, and dozens of dead and wounded were taken to hospital in buses. According to the official death toll, forty-six people died fighting in Ostankino alone.

Yeltsin declared a state of emergency in Moscow. He ordered the parliament building to be seized, and tanks opened fire on the White House. Russia was now back down to just one president. It was a pyrrhic victory for Russian democracy.

The troubles were not going to end anytime soon. On the contrary, it was only the beginning of the new era of turmoil.

Yeltsin's reformers were looking at Russia through a prism of economic theories and terms from the Western world, which they thought were universal and could be applied anywhere. The Russian Marxists had stepped on that particular rake before; now, it was the liberal market economists. They thought that, by following the economists' prescribed treatment, Russia would be back on its feet within '500 days' (as Gaidar's economic programme was called). Yet the medicine was developed by Western political economists to treat the illnesses of societies that had a very different history. Trusting in the market's self-healing powers and an enforced Big Bang privatisation proved to be the wrong approach. They were treating the patient for a cold – but the patient was riddled with tumours. The fundamental tenet of medicine to 'do no harm' was ignored. Shock therapy might work for other market economies, but here it resulted in the instantaneous expropriation of the general populace.

The West followed the Russian 'reforms' with enthusiasm and hope. They only saw what they wanted to see. Their misunderstanding of what was happening had begun with Gorbachev, and snowballed from there.

What can only be called 'the cult of Gorbachev' clearly had nothing to do with Gorbachev as a person; rather, he personified their euphoria at a historic miracle: the 'Russian soul' had been liberated from the spell cast by communist witchcraft – there was no longer any need to be afraid of 'those over there'. The prince who had roused the sleeping princess that was Russian democracy with a kiss, saved the world from the threat of nuclear war and enabled the reunification of Germany was a shining light which, they hoped, would bring forth further miracles, and guide the Soviet Union towards Europe. Yet in reality, his intention was anything but to establish a democracy. The decrepit colossus was stumbling towards its end, and all Gorbachev wanted to do was halt the collapse. While the West hailed him as a reformer, he did everything in his power to put the brakes on democratic reforms and save the communist Soviet Union.

Misunderstanding followed misunderstanding. When the red flag flying above the Kremlin was taken down and the Russian tricolour raised, the West believed that the enemy would disappear along with the Soviet Union. They saw in it unequivocal proof that the end of grand narratives was nigh. It was now inevitable and beyond all doubt that Russia would let itself be embraced by the civilised world, that the country would witness the arrival of democracy and become a free-market economy – it was only a question of time.

When the 1991 coup was defeated, the West laboured under the illusion that Russia would actually institute economic reforms leading to the creation of a free market, an illusion fed by young reformers such as Gaidar and Chubais. Their 'neoliberal' reforms sounded good, but the reality had nothing to do with those words. That is why these 'reforms' were so lauded by the West, and so hated in Russia.

The reforms amounted to the Party's former *nomenklatura* being recast as a new capitalist *nomenklatura*. The top ranks remained fundamentally the same. In the new 'capitalist' social order, the elite of the old communist society was still in charge. The big question for the Party's *nomenklatura* was how to cash in on their privileges and pass them on to their children. In a system where private ownership came without guarantees and where distribution was tightly controlled, it would be impossible. The crème de la crème of Soviet society dreamt of turning the state assets they had merely managed into their hereditary private property – which is precisely what happened during the wave of privatisation. With hindsight, perestroika and the entire transformation of the Soviet Union have been unmasked as a successful special operation on the part of the communist *nomenklatura*, designed to convert absolute political power into immense private wealth and the unrestricted power of money.

Just like the original version, the Soviet incarnation of the Moscow ulus was based on unconditional serfdom. Everyone, no matter what their rank, belonged to the state and the Great Khan, body and soul. Now, however, a small but powerful social group emerged which was independent from the state, and in fact could compel the state to act in its interests, and hit the Moscow ulus where it hurt. It was a seminal, historic transformation comparable to Peter III's emancipation of the nobility in 1762. The *nomenklatura* turned into a 'nouveau riche' aristocratic class that controlled estates (the former kolkhozes), businesses and natural resources, together with their peasant collectives and personnel. The richest of them formed a special caste: the oligarchs.

When the 'common people' were liberated (they didn't have to wait another hundred years this time), they were given no property of their own, just as in 1861. History was repeating itself. Personal freedom alone was of little value to Soviet workers. They were disappointed by their 'liberation' and thought the government had hoodwinked them. The result was the 1993 Moscow revolt.

The rebellion's bloody defeat put an end to the dialogue that had only just started, between the state and the people of the new Russia. The willingness of the 'red-brown' opposition to use violence, and those tanks firing on the parliament building, hardly made for fertile soil where a culture of compromise, indispensable to democracy, could grow.

Sham socialism was replaced by sham democracy. Overnight, loyal and selfless communists became imposing bankers, and convinced atheists converted into pious churchgoers (the Church taking up its old role of comforting the people and legitimising their rulers). The communist lie turned into a democratic lie. The people were now robbed to the sound of democratic slogans.

Those nouveau riche former functionaries divided Russia's natural resources among themselves, and rushed to sell them abroad. Ideally, any profit would remain in the West; why share their earnings with their fellow citizens? The whole country became one massive battlefield, with rival business gangs clashing fiercely over the distribution of resources.

The state claimed that Russia was heading for a democratic social order, but at every step the goal retreated further. Many of the early reformers soon lost any hope of establishing a state based on principles of democracy and justice, and joined either the opposition or the corrupt political mafia.

Russia's civil society was still in its infancy, but the potential middle class was already shrinking. For one thing, scientists, other highly educated specialists and IT experts were emigrating en masse to the West; for another, the population grew so rapidly impoverished that the social basis for democratic reform was reduced almost overnight. Have-nots are easier to manipulate with radical populist slogans.

The new era of turmoil had arrived. Chaos and lawlessness spread, and the people were sick of adventures in reform. Criminal gangs terrorised the country, and corruption proliferated. There was no such thing as scarce goods now – the shelves were full, only ordinary people couldn't get a ticket to this festival of consumption. While some flaunted their ill-gotten gains, others lacked the bare essentials.

The Soviet Union was cleaned out. The people were living among the ruins of an empire. Russia had lost its greatness; the deprivation remained. For most, life among the ruins of the empire was pointless and unpleasant. The majority fared badly on the unfettered 'free' market. The country grew depressed and forlorn. Over the course of generations, the state had taken from the people everything they had, and by way of compensation allowed them to feel proud of being the citizens of a vast and glorious country. Their thinking was done for them, decisions were made on their behalf, they were led. Now they felt the same emptiness professional soldiers feel when they are discharged from service. They were suddenly forced to take responsibility for their own lives, make their own way, do all their own thinking. The people missed the old certainties, the old order, the guiding hand of the authorities. That is the definition of Russian melancholy: a yearning for a defined world view, clear front lines, a distinct 'us' and 'them', a wise, paternal leader, a great victory, the homeland's old breadth and grandeur.

Widespread disappointment at the reforms and democracy itself infected the whole society with cynicism. People began to suspect that selfish motives and nefarious purposes lay behind all the beautiful big words: regardless what anyone said, they were driven only by self-interest, greed, vanity and egotism. Everyone kept quoting George Bernard Shaw's famous comment that democracy is 'a big balloon, filled with gas or hot air, and sent up so that you shall be kept looking up at the sky whilst other people are picking your pockets'. Every corner of society was now in the grip of cynicism.

Illusions dissipated. They fermented into an acrid vinegar that caused the erosion of values. The masses concluded that all officials were corrupt, that all people's deputies, ministers, police officers, generals, judges, principals, etc. took bribes and treated the state's coffers like their personal wallet, and that you couldn't believe or trust anyone. To protect your interests, you had to be rich or have useful connections in the criminal world. There was nothing else for it.

The desire to live in an orderly world expressed itself as Soviet nostalgia. The tsarist monarchy was idealised in Soviet times, and the same thing happened with the Soviet Atlantis when it went under. The people were exhausted by the chaos and lawlessness of 'democratic transformations', and longed for order. They blamed democracy for their plight, and the word itself became a swear word: instead of *'demokratiya'*, they said *'dermokratiya'*, a simple *r* turning a wonderful concept into 'shitocracy'.

My father talked that way too. When he died in 1995, he felt embittered and dejected. War veterans were particularly pained by the events; they had won the war, but lost the peace. My father was offended when the TV stations started depicting a wholly new version of the past. It turned out that he had fought against Hitler for a fascist regime that was even worse. All of a sudden, they were saying that, rather than helping to free other countries, he had helped to redeliver them into slavery. He drank so much, especially towards the end, that you wondered how his body could take it. He was impatient to join his dead friends. I think that when he did, order was restored to his world: he and his comrades were no longer occupiers, they were again the heroes who had saved their homeland and half of Europe from fascism.

My father, as well as millions of other people, ordinary Russians, sought stability and prosperity, but the 'shitocracy' was unable to provide them. The country's needs were reflected by the core ideas of the historical Moscow ulus: authoritarian policies, a strong state, a strict system. The powers that be in the Kremlin wanted to live up to people's expectations – which is how the First Chechen War came about.

After the USSR dissolved, fourteen former 'union republics'

(Ukraine, Belarus, Kazakhstan, Moldova, the Baltic states, and the republics in the Caucasus and Central Asia) declared their independence. By doing so, they reduced Russian territory to the borders of the mid-seventeenth-century Muscovite realm. What was Russia now? It still encompassed many different nations. Officially, it was called the Russian Federation; in reality, it was anything but: a 'federation' implies a voluntary partnership of nations and regions, but the events in Chechnya revealed just what kind of a partnership this was.

In 1991, the Chechens declared their exit from the 'voluntary' and 'democratic' Russian Federation. The other people's republics didn't dare follow suit. They were scared, and with good reason. Many urban Russian gangs were run by criminal organisations in the North Caucasus, particularly Chechnya. A single blow to the renegade republic would solve two problems at once: it would be an unequivocal public declaration of war on crime, and a lesson to other nations thinking of withdrawing from the Russian Federation. At the same time, a small, successful war would ensure that the Russian government no longer appeared weak in the eyes of the people.

The war evoked different reactions in the two 'Russian peoples': one wanted to stop the country from breaking up and to destroy the 'nest of criminals' once and for all. They supported tough military intervention, particularly when the TV stations started broadcasting daily images of the burnt and mutilated bodies of Russian soldiers. The other went on anti-war demonstrations.

The then defence minister Pavel Grachev publicly promised Yeltsin that, with the help of a single parachute regiment, he would take control of Grozny within two hours. The war lasted two years, claimed tens of thousands of lives – many of them civilians – and ended in Russia's defeat.

Given all its tanks and fighter jets, the Russian army's defeat at the hands of the little mountain republic's freedom fighters (Chechnya is 17,300 square kilometres in size, smaller than Wales) gave people an even greater sense of national humiliation. In Russia, a lost war has always been interpreted as an acute symptom that the system is diseased. It is a tsar's job to show strength; a weak tsar is a bad omen.

Yeltsin, a former member of the Communist Party's Central Committee and Politburo, only acted like a staunch democrat when in the process of seizing power. It is in great part thanks to him that democratic ideas became discredited in Russia. This 'democratic' president's actions boiled down to keeping his corrupt gang – the so-called 'family', in which his daughter was the key figure – in power.

The era of turmoil went on and on. 'The victory of democracy' of October 1993 in reality signalled the birth of a new monarchy. The monarch was already in place – but he turned out to be the wrong one. An old alcoholic with a heart condition, who had lost the war against the 'Chechen bandits' and handed the country over to be plundered by boyar oligarchs (in tsarist Russia, boyars were the class of aristocrats below the rank of a tsar or prince) did not meet society's expectations.

The country had become a mono-anarchy of sorts, and the people wanted order to be restored and to see their humiliated fatherland 'rise from its knees'. You clearly sensed that society was hoping for a new leader with a fist of iron.

Time was running out. The political mafia wanted to settle the question of Yeltsin's successor to their own advantage. The highest-ranking criminal gang in the country, the 'family', needed guarantees that the new lord of the Kremlin would safeguard their privileges. Operation Heir was firing on all cylinders. Various players were considered for the role of the new tsar – someone strong and fair for the ordinary ranks, someone pliable and reliable for the boyars. What they were after was a grey mouse, tame and easy to manipulate. As things turned out, the audition was won by a man who came from a litter of rats.

Chapter 5

Rising from Its Knees

After the Kremlin's *yarlyk* was handed over in 1999, Russian life proceeded in line with the textbooks once written by KGB professors for secret service agents – that is, it was characterised by provocations, electoral fraud, bribes, kompromat, media witch hunts, dirty political strategies, covert poisonings, public executions, hybrid wars, and more.

The country was released for 'special operations'. A small, successful war had proved an effective method – all you had to do was make sure you didn't lose. The FSB (the KGB's successor) made sure that the debut was a success. In September 1999, a wave of explosions rocked residential buildings in Moscow and other Russian cities. The attack caused outrage; 293 people died when the apartment blocks collapsed and more than a thousand were injured. The former FSB chief, Prime

Minister Putin, claimed that Chechen terrorists were responsible for the attacks. It was the excuse he needed to start the Second Chechen War. People were scared, and wholeheartedly welcomed the war on terror. Twelve months earlier, no one knew who he was; now, Putin took to the stage as Russia's saviour.

Granted, the residents of one apartment block in Ryazan caught his men red-handed in the basement with explosives, but the official explanation was that they'd been involved in 'exercises'. The Duma representative Sergei Yushenkov and the well-known journalist Yuri Shchekochikhin, who had demanded a public inquiry, died shortly afterwards. The former was shot dead outside his apartment building, the latter allegedly succumbed to 'toxic epidermal necrolysis'.

A brutal and deadly steamroller worked its way across Chechnya. The country was practically destroyed. As many as 200,000 people are estimated to have died. Following this genocide, in 2003, the republic held a referendum. Officially, 95.5 per cent of people voted to remain in the Russian Federation.

This is how Russia began to 'rise from its knees'. The Germans once wanted to quickly forget the 'humiliation at Versailles'; the Russians now wanted to quickly forget the break-up of the Soviet Union, the 'greatest geopolitical catastrophe of the twentieth century'.

One of the first things Putin did when he became president was to resurrect the old Soviet national anthem, which was introduced by Stalin in 1943 and dropped in 1991. Its author,

Sergei Mikhalkov, who had both written the hymn's original lyrics ('Stalin raised us') and reworked them under Brezhnev (replacing Stalin with 'the infallible Party'), now produced a third version ('Russia – our sacred state'), and the army was handed back the red Soviet banner with its Soviet star.

The new tsar promised people what they wanted: stability, order and a great empire. Before our very eyes, the Russia of the 'wild nineties' curdled into a new empire like milk into cottage cheese.

The twentieth century had witnessed the crumbling of the last of the world's empires; the largest of them, the British, officially ceased to exist in 1997, with Hong Kong's handover to China. Mankind entered the twenty-first century almost free of this historical burden. Only Russia played the spoilsport, despite the fact that its empire tried to break apart twice in the twentieth century – in 1917 and 1991. Yet both times, the process of decay was only half completed. Again and again, the Moscow ulus discovered the inner resources it needed to be reborn in a new guise. Amalrik, the man who predicted the dissolution of the Soviet Union back in the 1960s, had written: 'The Roman Empire's adoption of Christianity prolonged its lifespan by three hundred years, and the adoption of communism has prolonged the lifespan of the Russian empire by several decades.'

At the start of the new millennium, the ulus adopted a new avatar. The clear-cut ideological messages put out by past incarnations of the Moscow ulus, such as 'Orthodoxy, autocracy, nationality' and 'Workers of the world, unite!', were replaced by hybrid catchphrases tailored to the new era: 'the dictatorship of law', the 'institutional vertical of power' and 'managed democracy'. The outcome was the same. The messianic vision was reduced to the claim that Russia was the last bastion of moral principles, of traditional, national, cultural, religious and even sexual values, which the West had lost. For the Russian people, it was more than enough – and 'Gayropa' would in any case never really get 'our spirituality'.

Everything the people ached for during the turmoil of the 1990s was returned to them via TV propaganda. The world became black-and-white. They were told that the era of turmoil, when Russia was chastened by the West, was over. The president, they were told, had helped the country to rise like a phoenix from the ashes. Russia had 'risen from its knees' to be once more on a par with the West. The conflict with the West, they were told, was a conflict of values. More or less the whole world had succumbed to the chief evildoer, and only Russia, led by the topless strongman with the muscular torso, could stand up to the US.

Ancient Egyptians believed that the pharaoh was the son of the sun god and the living incarnation of Horus. They thought the world was made up of two halves: the black earth, i.e. Egypt, was ruled by the pharaoh, alias Horus, god of the heavens and the sun; the other half, the red desert, belonged to Seth, god of chaos, war and death. This world view was implanted into the skulls of Russia's inhabitants every evening, for years: the black earth was the sacred Rus, their president the living pharaoh; the red desert was the West, which sowed war and death.

A dictatorship cannot exist without the cult of the dictator. Rudolf Hess's famous words, 'Hitler is Germany, as Germany is Hitler!' were repeated almost word for word by the chairman of the Duma, when he said that 'Putin is Russia. There is no Russia without Putin. Any attack on Putin is an attack on Russia.'

Putin is sacred because the state is sacred. In the Russian Church, all sacred acts are conducted behind closed altar doors. The profane people have no access to the sanctum sanctorum. The sacraments of power are dispensed in exactly the same way, behind closed doors. The state is divided from the people by an iconostasis, and surrounded by secrecy. This is why the dictator's private life is shrouded in secrecy too – a Stalin or a Putin is not married to some mere mortal or other, but to Russia.

It is intrinsically impossible for the Russian state to be open and transparent. As in the old days, we can only surmise what is happening in that black box behind the walls of the Kremlin, and how decisions are made there. Any communication between the Kremlin and the profane world happens via signals. You wait for the secret signal, seeking coded revelations in public statements.

It is an empire's victories and defeats that reveal whether the tsar is real, or whether an impostor is sitting on the throne. Yeltsin was not loved by the Russian god. He could not even bring the Chechens to heel. Putin, though, is real, and even the rise in oil prices was a clear sign that his power was blessed. The billions that rained down from the heavens during the early 2000s brought relative wealth to Russia, and were seen as unequivocal proof that the iron fist that had replaced the 'shitocracy' with the 'vertical of power' ruled by the grace of God.

In the pantheon of the third Russian empire sit the saints of the two preceding ones, the tsarist and the Soviet empires. Both Nicholas II and Felix Dzerzhinsky, the founder of the Russian secret service, are idolised. Yet this creates no cognitive dissonance, despite the fact that Dzerzhinsky epitomises the tyranny that counted the last tsar and his family among its victims. Really, this should be the cause of confusion and a fractured consciousness: the revolution, the downfall of the monarchy, children shot dead – all are condemned as evil, but the leader of the organisation responsible for the murders is acclaimed as a 'superb statesman'. Only outsiders notice a flaw in the logic of this simultaneous reverence shown to both victim and killer. In Russia, they see nothing contradictory in idolising both, because here they celebrate the cult of power as such. Nicholas was the tsar, the symbol of power, so you had to pay homage to him, not depose – let alone kill – him. Dzerzhinsky served those in power and shielded them from their enemies; he was therefore not an executioner or a murderer, but an exemplary subject. When it comes to safeguarding whoever is in power, anything goes. At school, our teachers told us that the tsar's children could have become the White Army's living banner, and were thus a threat to the new regime – so they obviously had to be killed.

It was not only for the top job that the secret service provided the personnel. In the new hierarchy, almost every high-ranking post was filled with former KGB officers. The KGB once formed the core of the apparatus of oppression, terrorising the people, hunting down dissidents, persecuting anyone who dared to think freely and putting pressure on the Russian Orthodox Church. Those who rule Russia today spent their previous careers attacking the very same national values whose uncompromising defenders they now claim to be.

In the new Russia, the FSB-KGB-NKVD-Cheka is the pride of the nation. The murderous organisation's centenary was celebrated lavishly; in his ceremonial address to his colleagues, the president declared, 'No matter how much times change, the vast majority of people who choose this difficult career have always been true supporters of the state and patriots. They performed their duties with dignity and honesty, and put the fatherland and the people first.' In other words, the Lubyanka (the unofficial name for the secret service) has always served the people. Executions and mass murders are expressions of patriotism, dignity and professional integrity. There is no need to do penance. We should be proud of our past.

Can you imagine a German chancellor declaring after the war that the Gestapo were 'patriots' who 'performed their duties with dignity and integrity, and put the fatherland and the people first', and that everyone should be proud of them? The Germans spent decades learning to recover from Hitler's fascism; in the new Russia, they are pulling out all the stops in their cultivation of Stalinist fascism. That is how the Russian version of 'coming to terms with history' operates.

The first and most important reform implemented by the new 'dictatorship of law' was to weaken the oligarchs and relieve them of their assets. People who had only recently come into possession of vast riches were demoted to servile managers of their own wealth. They nominally retained their shares and title deeds, but only for as long as they showed loyalty to the Great Khan. Anyone who showed discontent soon learnt their lesson. Some, like Vladimir Gusinsky and Boris Berezovsky, feared arrest and fled abroad. The former retired to Spain, the latter tried to get involved in politics and was later found hanged at his Berkshire estate. The case of Mikhail Khodorkovsky was meant to serve as a vivid example: the oligarch had to do ten years' penance in the Gulag for standing up to the diktats of the state, and by breaking up his company, Yukos, the state demonstrated to the whole world that there was no such thing as private ownership or independent courts in Russia. But without these two pillars, the 'normal' type of market economy common in the West can't exist.

Private ownership is inherently impossible in the ulus, because it results in a collision between two spheres of power: the power that an individual exercises over their private property inevitably ends up at odds with the one and only power at the top of the pyramid. Here, 'private property' isn't property, but granted to you merely provisionally as reward for your loyalty. The moment you lose the trust of whoever is in power, you are likely to lose your property along with it. This robust system of personal allegiance to your superiors forms the backbone of the regime. It was exactly the same in the Soviet Union, where your allegiance to communist ideals was no substitute for your devotion to your boss, the source of all favour and harm. When a provincial ulus overlord obtained a better position in Sarai, his vassals would follow him with all their goods and chattels. Thus Putin, too, moved to Moscow with his Leningrad entourage in tow.

The freshly established 'institutional vertical of power' is nothing other than a strict chain of command, a principle in which the Russians are well versed. The true meaning of democratic institutions such as parliaments, constitutions and courts has been reduced to a fig leaf. Everyone knows that the parliament is really the ruler's bodyguard, that his wish list is the country's real constitution, and that the judges serve anything but the law. It is with good reason that people say, 'The law is like a cart – wherever you point the shafts, there it goes.'

The political system's democratic packaging meets the highest standards, but the contents smack of the ulus. The presidential elections are an opportunity for the subjects to prove their loyalty. You are free to cast your vote for the Great Khan, in the knowledge that refusing to do so won't change the pyramid of power. The results are falsified anyway. Stalin once said, 'What is important is not how they vote, but who counts the votes, and how.' The same is true of all other elections in Russia. Fictitious voters take part in fictitious elections for a fictitious Duma. Duma elections and local elections are basically pointless; all they do is mirror domestic politics, which constitutes nothing more than powerful people fighting over a piece of the pie. Ordinary voters are allowed to approach the ballot box, but not the pie.

Several parties are represented in the Duma; but there are no parties. There is no contradiction here either. The people have learnt their lesson from the GDR and its multi-party system, where all parties served the same ruler – the occupying Soviet power. The same is true of the new Russia, and the only advantage here is that the occupying power and the people speak the same language.

This is what the pyramid of power looks like in Russia today: at the top – well, we know who's at the top. On the next step down are the so-called *siloviki* (from *sila*, 'force', 'strength'), the higher-ranking spooks and military leaders. They are the ones who maintain order in the empire, and they are immensely powerful. On the level below them are the tamed oligarchs, followed by the deputies and officials. Together, they form a sort of military state structure. After that come the rank and file.

The glue that holds the edifice together has stood the test of time, and works flawlessly – that glue is fear. The modern version of dictatorship doesn't need mass purges: just as, in the twenty-first century, carpet bombing has been replaced by 'smart' weapons, so the regime no longer needs the Gulag. Targeted arrests and assassinations suffice. All you have to do is arrest a minister or a famous theatre director under the pretext of the 'war against corruption' to send an unequivocal message to the other ministers and theatre directors. The murders of the journalist Anna Politkovskaya and opposition politician Boris Nemtsov sent just such a clear message to the disaffected. Their names became famous in the West, but hundreds of lesser-known victims have been crippled, tortured, thrown into prison and murdered in an effort to intimidate the subjects.

When the criminal code has an article for everything a citizen might or might not do, no matter what, mass executions are redundant. The law and financial regulations are so confusing and contradictory that every single inhabitant of the country feels like a criminal. In a democratic society, everything that is not expressly forbidden in law is allowed. In the ulus, no one knows what is allowed and what is forbidden, because it can change from one moment to the next. There are laws, yet there are none, because the only law is the will of those who wield power. The courts are there to execute that will. Selective justice is one of tyranny's latest tactics.

For the twenty-first-century dictatorship, open borders are a groundbreaking new tactical device. The regime appears to have studied its predecessors closely in an effort to avoid repeating their mistakes. I grew up in a twentieth-century dictatorship. The reason the entire country was behind barbed wire is that we were the empire's slaves, and the empire needed us. Today's system is built on oil and gas exports, so it has no use for the general population: why should the masters share their profits with the riff-raff? This is why the borders are open, and anyone who isn't happy is unambiguously asked to leave the country. Open borders are a successful tactic in the regime's endeavour to reduce the social grounds for active internal opposition. In the age of Putin, millions have left the country, or are about to. The numbers are rising sharply. They are mainly tertiary educated, engineers, scientists, IT experts – i.e. the nation's true elite. The regime is robbing Russia not only of its natural resources, but also of its human capital, and thus failing to invest in the country's future. This catastrophic loss of people is weakening the country, but shoring up the dictatorship.

Once more, the empire is staging its old drama for three actors – the silent people, the democratic opposition and the state. Today, nearly thirty years after the 'liberation of the serfs', the overwhelming majority of Russia's inhabitants still don't have a passport, and have never been abroad. They don't have enough money for a trip to the West. The two 'Russian nations' live cheek by jowl on the same streets, but in parallel realities. The majority of Russians are mentally still in the Middle Ages, and believe the zombie box that is television when it tells them that the holy fatherland is surrounded by enemies. The rest, however, are too well travelled, too well read and have surfed the web too much. In short, free travel and exchange of information with the West have dealt my homeland the same old nasty trick. The democratic virus is highly contagious, and the educated are particularly susceptible to it, because education inevitably leads to thoughts of human dignity. These Russians take to the streets and believe that Putin and his henchmen belong in prison; for the other Russians, the state is sacred and untouchable. The former believe that the country has to be led out of the bloody swamp that is Russian history, and towards a liberal European system. For the latter, only a tsar with a fist of iron can guarantee order.

In 2011, Moscow's streets and squares witnessed the 'White Revolution', when the emerging civil society openly declared war on the regime. I spent that year in Russia. When the prime minister and the president shamelessly swapped places on the chessboard and the parliamentary elections were rigged, the situation suddenly exploded. It took just a few days for Moscow to wake up. What followed was a peaceful civilian revolution: a Russian Spring in midwinter. They called it the 'White Revolution' because the people wore white ribbons as a sign of non-violent protest. A middle class had emerged in the big cities, where people had learnt how to survive 'unfettered' capitalism: they solved their financial problems without help from the state, lived in a highly competitive environment, and managed to secure an adequate standard of life for their families. The seeds had sprouted almost invisibly, below ground, and now, suddenly, grass was growing everywhere. From one day to the next, Russian society was no longer willing to submit to the government's degrading ways. It had grown up, and outgrown the nappies of authoritarianism. Russian citizens were becoming increasingly self-confident. They saw themselves no longer as small cogs in the colossal state machinery, but as something akin to Western-style individual taxpayers who wanted to cooperate with the state.

Marching through the streets with thousands of like-minded people was as wonderful then as it had been twenty years earlier. In that winter of 2011, it seemed like most of Moscow was with us, and that we would win. I rather liked this Moscow! It felt so good to see and experience that other, democratic Russia. Our revolution wasn't a senseless, violent mutiny, as the regime's supporters claimed on TV. They were trying to intimidate people, but not a single violent incident occurred during the mass protests. For the first time, a Russian revolt was proceeding sensibly and soberly. A peaceful revolution was happening in Russia; it was an opportunity for us to leave the railway tracks of mutiny and dictatorship, and turn onto the road to change. It became clear to me that people need revolutions to feel human again. People need those moments, when they refuse to be demeaned any longer and take to the streets to defend their personal dignity. 'We are the power,' we chanted again. The Kremlin thought otherwise.

In 1917, and again when perestroika arrived, the powers that were handed in their resignation. This time, though, the *siloviki* mentality behind the red wall won out: there would be no withdrawal. As 'managed democracy' unfolded, the screws were tightened further and further. The opposition was publicly denounced as a fifth column acting for the West, and employees of the remaining independent civil organisations were defamed as 'foreign agents' and ejected from the political stage. The protests were violently dispersed, and people randomly arrested at rallies to intimidate the others.

The regime knows only one way to get the country under control: war. War is the magic bullet deployed by all dictatorships. The mass media became hysterically patriotic. 'We are at war,' said the propaganda machine. It said the West wanted to annihilate us, and that – like our fathers and grandfathers before us – we were prepared to sacrifice everything for the victory over fascism. Anyone who disagreed was a traitor. For a dictatorship, what is important is not specific military actions, but the mere fact that there is a war, the condition of war as such, because it gives the regime licence to ostracise and persecute its enemies as traitors.

The leadership played the nationalist card. The watchword was '*Russkiy mir*' – the Russian world. Even the Russian language was drafted into the Kremlin's service, as it sought to build a new Russian empire.

Following the break-up of the Soviet Union, almost overnight, twenty-five million Russians found themselves living in the 'near abroad'. In the Soviet republics' successor states, people from the 'occupying nation' were now in the minority and had to learn the language of the relevant dominant ethnicity. They felt marginalised in the hierarchy of the new nation states. It was a traumatic experience for them; most had to reorganise their lives wholesale, and were suddenly second-class citizens.

These people now became the Kremlin's own 'fifth column'. Just as Germans once said, 'Wherever we are, that's where Germany is,' the Russian president now announced: 'Russia has no borders. Russia does not end anywhere.' The nationalist rhetoric dispensed by the propaganda broadcasts on TV seemingly came straight from Hitler's *Mein Kampf*, except that 'German' was substituted for 'Russian' using Word's find-and-replace function.

The 'near abroad' wasn't a comfortable place to be. The post-Soviet world tried anything and everything to uncouple from the old mother state. Kazakhstan gave up Cyrillic script and adopted the Latin alphabet, and the Baltic republics managed to cover themselves with the 'NATO shield'. Ukraine did what it could to extract itself from the Kremlin's grip – but Crimea was its Achilles heel.

And so Ukraine became the target of Russian propaganda. The fact that the republic turned its back on close economic collaboration with Russia was blamed on the machinations of the US, which had thereby extended its sphere of influence all the way to the Russian border. The newly independent state's demands that all citizens learn the national language and use Ukrainian in public contexts was presented as debasing and oppressing the Russians who lived there. Russian TV stations injected into the collective consciousness a yearning for the return of Crimea, which would signal the fatherland's restoration to its former size and glory.

Crimea thus replaced Constantinople in Russia's sacred mythology. Dostoevsky once wrote that 'a truly great people can never reconcile itself to playing second fiddle in the affairs of humanity', that 'there is only one nation among all nations that can have the true God ... And the only "god-bearing" people is the Russian people'.* In *A Writer's Diary*, he recorded a discussion with Nikolai Danilevsky during the Russo-Turkish war of 1877–78 about the fate of Constantinople – Danilevsky was a pan-Slavist, and thought that Constantinople should become the capital of all Slavs after its liberation, including the Russians. This angered Dostoevsky: 'What kind of comparison between the Russians and the Slavs can there be here?' he asks. 'Constantinople must be *ours*, conquered by *us*, the Russians, from the Turks, and it must remain ours for ever.'†

Putin's empire is much smaller than the empire of the Romanovs was, and is proportionally less presumptuous: rather than bringing about the Third Rome by conquering the Second Rome, they presented the masses with something neat and catchy: that a drunk Khrushchev had handed 'our' Crimea over to the Ukrainians, and that it was time to right this historical

---

* *The Devils*, trans. David Magarshack (Harmondsworth: Penguin, 1971), p. 258.
† *A Writer's Diary, Volume Two: 1877–1881*, trans. Kenneth Lantz (Evanston, IL: Northwestern University Press), pp. 1207–8.

injustice. Crimea was sacred Russian land, it was where Christianity first entered Russia. Crimea had to be ours, conquered by us, the Russians, from the Ukrainians, and it had to remain ours for ever.

After such intense brainwashing, the people were ready for the coming war on the neighbouring state. The state told them that Ukrainian fascists were oppressing our brothers, and that we would not desert them. 'Russians don't abandon their own,' went the rallying cry. The general staff merely waited until the Winter Olympics were over before deploying its so-called 'little green men'. A wave of popular patriotic enthusiasm was assured.

When the Soviet empire collapsed, the people of my country had a unique opportunity to reshape their lives, to make their own decisions and transform the country into a wonderful home. But all they did was build new barracks.

As we looked on, Russia emigrated from the twenty-first century to the Middle Ages.

When someone is born and grows up in a prison camp, the barbed wire never leaves their soul. Having your freedom restored by the powers that be is not enough – you need to remove the barbed wire from your very soul.

In March 2013, before the annexation of Crimea and before the war against Ukraine, I published an open letter in Russia. The Federal Press and Mass Communication Agency, i.e. the Russian 'Ministry of Truth', had invited me to join an official delegation of Russian writers attending the BookExpo America trade fair in New York. I knew that, once the letter was published, the propaganda machine would declare me a Russian traitor and that I would be subjected to a witch hunt. Which is exactly what happened. But I thought it was important not to stay silent. Silence is complicity.

This is what I wrote:

The political course of Russia and the events of recent years have created a situation in the country that is absolutely unacceptable and degrading to its people and its great culture. As a Russian and a Russian citizen, I am ashamed of the events in my country. If I take part in a book fair as a member of an official delegation and profit from the opportunities that it presents me with as an author, it means being at the same time duty-bound to represent a state whose politics I consider damaging to the country, and an official system that I find abhorrent.

A country where a criminal and corrupt regime has seized power, where the state is a hierarchy of criminals, where elections have transformed into a farce, where the courts serve those in power and not the law, where there are political prisoners, where state TV has prostituted itself, where the usurpers enact reams of insane laws that result in society regressing back to the Middle Ages – a country like that cannot be my Russia. I cannot and will not be a member of an official Russian delegation that represents this Russia.

I want to, and shall, represent a different Russia, my Russia, a country freed from its usurpers, a country whose public authorities protect not the right to be corrupt but the rights of the individual, a country with a free media, free elections and a free people.

My mother is Ukrainian, my father Russian. There are millions of such mixed marriages in Russia and Ukraine. Sometimes I am glad that they aren't around to witness this war between Russia and Ukraine.

We are brother nations. How can you disentangle our common ignominy and our common grief – our terrible history? How can you disentangle the annihilation of Russia's peasantry from Ukraine's Great Famine, the Holodomor? The victims included both Russians and Ukrainians – as did the mass murderers. We had a common enemy – ourselves. Our terrible past has both nations in its lethal grip and is refusing to let us go into the future.

A common history also means a common culture. How can you separate it, how bisect its living body? How can you carve up Nikolai Gogol? Is he a classic of Russian or Ukrainian literature? Gogol belongs to us both, he is a source of pride for us both.

It is cruel villainy to set our people against one another. In recent years, I have been tortured by shame over my country. I am now just as ashamed of the new Russia as I was once ashamed of the Soviet Union as a young man. The patriot-in-chief in the Kremlin doesn't feel things like that, he has nothing but contempt for both Ukrainians and Russians. And for the rest of the world. This is what all dictators in history have in common: they want to live for ever – and if they can't, the rest of the world will have to go down with them.

What was so surprising about the Maidan Uprising was the civil courage shown by the people who took to the streets 'for your and our freedom'. Their mutual solidarity was striking. In Russia, many people responded with admiration and jealousy: the Ukrainians were able to rise up and persist – it was harder to bring *them* to their knees.

On Russian TV, the people's revolution was maligned as a Western secret service conspiracy. They said that NATO had attacked us via Ukraine, and that we had to defend ourselves.

Initially, Putin's TV presenters pulled out all the stops to make the Maidan's defenders look like provincial Russian clots: cunning, miserly, stupid, and happy to sell themselves to the devil or even to the West – as long as there was enough bacon in the house.

There has always been a certain condescending attitude towards Ukrainians and the Ukrainian language in Russia. The 'little brother' is praised for his *joie de vivre*, sense of humour and self-deprecation, but he remains the junior member of the family. As such, he must obey his older brother, learn from him and emulate him. The Maidan Uprising revealed a very different Ukrainian people. All of a sudden, the little brother was more mature than his big brother. We haven't managed to eject our criminal gang yet, but the Ukrainians have managed to eject theirs.

The Ukrainian president was scared of blood – the Russian president was not. Crimean Berkut units (a police force reporting directly to the Ministry of Internal Affairs) fired into the crowd, evidently already following orders from Moscow rather than Kyiv. They were later integrated with the Moscow OMON troops.

The Maïdan Uprising prevailed. Russian TV changed its rhetoric: now the Ukrainians were brutal Nazis and SS devotees. It was high time, they said, to save the Russian-speaking population in Ukraine from genocide.

The people in Crimea who were waving the Russian tricolour with tears in their eyes yelling, 'Russia! Russia!' were a sorry sight. As so often in history, they were being exploited and deceived. Their path to Russia led them directly into a criminal police state (in Russia, they don't consider such a thing an antinomy). Their enthusiasm for the 'historic liberation' from the Ukrainian 'fascists' didn't last long. Only a few years later, a sobering reality has set in. When Russia 'liberated' Abkhazia from Georgia, the once flourishing watering places on the Black Sea became deserted. The same scenario now awaited Crimea after its 'liberation'. This once lively holiday resort has become a grey spot that neither Russians nor Ukrainians want to visit. Anonymous troops occupied Crimea. Then, later, when the annexation was complete, Putin publicly admitted that the 'little green men' had been Russian special units. The peninsula's annexation produced hysterical cheers in Russia. The triumphant cry 'Crimea is ours!' carved a searing line through the Russian people. It ran through families, old friends no longer saw eye to eye, people stopped being able to explain things, to convince each other. For some, Crimea's return to the 'home port' was the new Russia's greatest victory and proudest moment; for others, it was a national disgrace.

The president now stood before his people as a 'gatherer of Russian soil', in the best tsarist tradition. The people were no longer silent. The people were beside themselves with joy: the tsar was real, victory was ours. It was about more than Crimea: they were celebrating Russia's victory over the US, the West, the whole world. The country wallowed in its freshly regained sense of importance.

When the then US secretary of state, John Kerry, said that Putin was behaving 'in a nineteenth-century fashion', he echoed what many people felt in the West. Yet why should the Kremlin care what century it was? The Moscow ulus had conquered time itself.

The glorious recovery of Crimea already has its own chapter in school textbooks, and the next chapter waiting in the wings will tell the story of how Kyiv crawled on its knees back into the arms of the Russian world, like the prodigal son.

Operation Novorossiya ('New Russia') was the next phase in the general staff's plans for the neighbouring state's dismemberment. Ten regions would be taken from Ukraine in the east and south, which would constitute the vassal ulus of Novorossiya. To that end, the propaganda machine created the attractive-sounding 'Russian Spring' brand. The special secret service operation would be sold to the public as a new patriotic war against fascism. The TV stations loaded the guns. Following a TV bulletin showing a refugee describing with tears in her eyes how the Ukrainian rabble of soldiers shot a mother and crucified her three-year-old boy in Sloviansk's main square, thousands volunteered to defend the minority Russians against the Ukrainians. Later, it turned out that the news bulletin had been staged, and was fake news. But war was already raging.

In the twenty-first century, a state can start a war without a formal declaration. The war criminals of Russian TV were sending young people into battle and to their deaths. They took up arms voluntarily, believing that they were fighting fascism, that they were virtuous Russian knights battling the evil West. Into their dingy lives among the ruins of the empire there had suddenly come an opportunity for them to perform noble deeds for a worthy goal. The lives of millions of Russians suddenly meant something again: they were building a Russian world, fighting on the side of good in the battle against the Western devil who had appeared in the shape of 'Ukrofascism' – 'Ukrainian fascism'.

The myth of the 'gathering of Russian soil' was reanimated before our very eyes. The resurrection of the vast empire was declared the highest purpose of the Russian people, which was finally rising from its knees after being fractured by defeat in the Cold War, the break-up of the Soviet Union and the unfairness with which the borders were subsequently redrawn. The supporters of the 'Russian Spring' weren't fighting for the separation of Donbas from Ukraine, but for Ukraine's reunification with the empire. In the eyes of these imperialists, the Ukrainians are separatists. In the programmatic words of Alexander Borodai, the chief ideologist and first prime minister of Putin's new Russia, 'Russia's borders extend far beyond the borders of the Russian Federation. I am leading a historic mission in the name of the Russian nation, which is a supra-ethnicity bound together by Orthodox Christianity. For there is only one Russia, the illustrious Russia, the Russian empire, and that's why the Ukrainian separatists sitting in Kyiv are fighting against the Russian empire.'

In the minds and souls of millions of Russians, the ulus has won once again. It's much nicer to believe that you are on a historic mission than to vegetate away among the ruins of the empire.

Lead-lined coffins – code-named 'Cargo 200' – arrived in Russia from Donbas. You can tell how a fatherland cares for its children from how it buries its heroes. Once upon a time, the parents of those who died in Afghanistan were prohibited from marking the place of death on the grave-stone; today, they bury Russian soldiers and officers who have fallen in Ukraine the same way – secretly. And they do so willingly.

The Kremlin is doing all it can to keep Kyiv out of Europe. With civil war and bloodshed, the regime has put the shackles on Ukraine. It is taking revenge on the people who truly tried to rise from their knees. The Kremlin will never allow a democratic Russian-speaking state to exist.

A successful independent Ukraine would represent an acute threat to the powers that be in Moscow, because it would send a clear signal to the Russian people. For the occupants of the Kremlin, the existence of such a Ukraine is – and this is no exaggeration – a matter of life and death. That's why they want to foment chaos in Ukraine, which would then send a different, albeit just as clear, signal to the Russian people: 'Look at the misery that democracy creates!'

They don't even make a secret of their strategy: the Moscow ulus wants to destabilise the deeply divided country of Ukraine – by means of subversive pro-Russian groups, economic pressure and its secret services – until the country descends into chaos and civil war. This scenario is the goal of the Russian leadership's operations in Ukraine. The only thing that can stand in their way is the people. Ukraine has a weak government, but a very strong civil society.

It is this strong civil society that caused Operation Novorossiya to fail. Russia's secret services only succeeded in sparking off the 'Russian Spring' in two of the ten regions. The *Russkiy mir* won in Luhansk and Donetsk, and now we can see what this 'Russian world' has done for the inhabitants of these self-proclaimed republics. The people innocently waited for Russia to help their ailing regions make a fresh start, but the Kremlin instead allowed eastern Ukraine to be stripped by gangs. Operation New Russia was a fiasco. The hopes and expectations of the people were betrayed, the inhabitants cruelly abused and abandoned. This is what the ulus always does. It can do no other. In the years since then, they could have turned Donbas into a shop window showcasing the Russian world – turned it into an attractive and inviting place for both Russians and Ukrainians. Instead, they built the only thing the Moscow ulus is capable of building: a bandits' lair.

The Kremlin will keep stoking the conflict in Donbas; sometimes it'll let it die down a little, sometimes it'll add fresh fuel to it. It will become an insoluble problem, like Gaza. The Great Khan will never give in – it would be taken as a sign of weakness, and Russians don't like weaklings. The rest of the world will accept this, and at some point go about its own business again. *De jure*, the Western democracies will never recognise the annexation of Crimea; but they have already done so *de facto*. There is nothing new under the sun. The Soviet Union once occupied three Baltic republics that were *de jure* never recognised by the US as part of the USSR, but this didn't cause any real issues between the two countries during the fifty years that followed. That's how it will be with Crimea too.

The West doesn't want to rouse the anger of its unpredictable Russian partner, who is prone to attacking other countries and showing off new weapons of mass destruction. The last thing the West wants to do is provoke a war. But the West has misread the situation: the Moscow ulus is already at war with it.

Russia and the West have been studying one another for centuries, but we can't see each other clearly. Something is wrong with the optics. All we see are mirror images.

Chapter 6

'The Window to Europe' – or a Mirror?

My grandparents and my parents were separated from Europe by a barbed-wire fence. When I was seventeen, London and Berlin might as well have been on another planet. Eating a croissant in a Paris café was unthinkable.

For us, there was no such thing as the West. We could scarcely credit the propaganda images that depicted life over there as unhappy, and over here as happy – all that waffling on TV merely drifted past our ears. The TV lot were trying to feed us a repulsive West of their own invention.

The most contrived of all Russian conceptions of the West is Nikolai Karamzin's portrayal of it as little short of a paradise, which originated in eighteenth-century depictions produced by German and French tutors employed on Russian estates thronging with slaves. Karamzin, conscientious student that he was, made Switzerland the emblem of that West. In *Letters of a Russian Traveller*, he describes how he dropped to his knees on the banks of the Rhine near Basel: 'Happy Swiss! Dwelling in sweet nature's embrace, under the beneficent laws of a brotherly union, with simple ways serving one God, do you not each day, each hour, thank Heaven for your good fortune?'*

Yet this 'enlightened' variation on the West was invented *ex negativo*. Whereas in Russia life is governed by the motto, 'If you're the boss, I'm the idiot; if I'm the boss, you're the idiot', over there they have things like republics, equality and elections. Whereas in Russia there's the saying, 'You can't build a stone chamber with honest work', in the West it's honest work that gets you your own little house 'with a stork on the roof' (Dostoevsky couldn't get that stork on the roof out of his head – in his novel *The Gambler*, it becomes a symbol for the petit-bourgeois West). Whereas in Russia something is yours only until someone stronger fancies taking it away from you, over there private ownership is sacred, and a farmer knows that his pastures will still belong to his family ten generations later; and so on, and so forth.

When I was young, Europe was a myth. Europe was a Russian dream of life lived with dignity. To us, Europe above all signified European values: the rights of the individual,

---

* N. M. Karamzin, *Letters of a Russian Traveler 1789–1790: An Account of a Young Russian Gentleman's Tour Through Germany, Switzerland, France, and England*, trans. and abridged by Florence Jonas (Westport, CT: Greenwood Press, 1976), p. 115.

the preservation of human dignity, freedom. For generations of educated people obscured by the Iron Curtain, Europe meant all the things that were denied to them. And it was because we wanted to open our country up to that Europe and affiliate ourselves with it, that we took to the streets in Moscow in 1991, and again twenty years later, in 2011. It is for this Europe that the Ukrainians campaigned in the Maidan, and for this Europe that the 106 women and men, the 'celestial hundred' who died during those violent clashes in January and February, gave their lives. Are the inhabitants of Brussels, Strasbourg or The Hague prepared to die for the European Union? I doubt it, because we are talking about different Europes. The concept of 'Europe' encompasses many different, overlapping meanings. For people living in Paris, Monaco or Berlin, it has come to represent a confluence of problems, financial crises, national debt and an all too powerful bureaucracy. It is the Europe of officials who tell farmers where and how to cultivate their fields. It is a fearful Europe, where people are afraid of drowning in the waves of refugees coming from Asia and Africa.

Over time, the idea of the 'common house of Europe' that filled its architects, the survivors of the Second World War, with such joy has evaporated. The same happens with every major new construction: once the house-warming party is over, the inhabitants gradually lose the ability to perceive what they have in common. Everyday problems and other issues make it impossible to be neighbourly, and drive a wedge between people who live next door to each other. After all, what can you expect from your neighbours? One litters the entrance, another makes too much noise at night, a third doesn't pay their rent, yet another zealously tries to restore order but only ends up getting on everyone's nerves – why should you love neighbours like that? Why should you love such a Europe? Its break-up is merely the natural consequence of centrifugal force. 'I don't want to go to Europe,' says Europe.

In Russia, too, it is a different kind of Europe for which we yearn. The same goes for the Ukrainians who marched to the Maidan. It is not for the European Union embodied by bureaucrats in Brussels, but for a life lived in dignity that they rose up against the criminal gangs that once plied their trade in Kyiv, and which are still in charge in Moscow. 'For your and our freedom!' The Great Khan in the Kremlin can't forgive Ukraine for that – and never will.

This is precisely why Russian TV equates the West with fascism and tens of millions of Russians believe that NATO is using Ukraine to wage war against Russia. The zombie box is drumming an unequivocal image into their heads: the West is the enemy, and Europe is equivalent to the fascism against which our grandfathers once fought, and from which we must now protect our homeland.

Hammering a 'window to Europe' into the wall is not enough (we have the Italian Francesco Algarotti and his 1760 book *Viaggi di Russia*, 'Travels in Russia', to thank for the phrase). When someone looks through the window, all they see is their own reflection. The two Russian peoples have two very different ideas of Europe: for one, Europe is their spiritual homeland, an atopia, a place that exists nowhere but which fascinates and attracts them, which promises freedom and human dignity; for the other, it is an ancient and eternal adversary, a 'hereditary enemy' who, led by the US, wants to enslave and, yes, even eradicate Russia. Likewise, when someone looks through the window from the other side, the Russia they see reflects the viewer. This is how the strange myth of the Russian soul came about, that mysterious, lost Russian soul, wandering about a boundless, untamed landscape searching for the essence of life, a noble savage as yet undefiled by civilisation and globalisation. They seek in Russian literature, music and art something that the West lost long ago: true spirituality, profundity, soulfulness.

The 'Russian soul' was, incidentally, coined by the Germans. By the time the Russians started pondering who they really were, the 'Russian soul' had been an established concept in 'Russian Studies' for two hundred years. It first appeared in a mid-seventeenth-century book by Adam Olearius about his sojourn in the Moscow empire, in which he describes an Orthodox church: 'Over the doors was depicted the Last Judgement . . . the monk showed us a person in German dress and said: "Germans and other peoples may be saved, too, if only their souls are Russian."'

The West was looking for an explanation for the Russians' otherness, their ability to persevere despite the horrors of their history, their singular, astonishing tolerance for suffering – they even spoke of the Russians' need to suffer, a 'Russian delight in suffering'. And when they couldn't find an explanation plausible enough from a European perspective, they attributed everything that Western minds could not grasp to a mysterious Russian soul that still drew strength from the sacred and the hidden – something long denied to the rational West by its healthy common sense and capacity for reason.

Russians obviously like hearing such flattering musings on the mysterious Russian soul. Clichés like that fit perfectly into the notion of the country as a 'wintry fairy tale'. When foreigners start talking about the notorious Russian soul, Russians nod – but among ourselves, we shrug. It has never puzzled us. Vasily Grossman put it best in his (once banned) 1961 novel *Everything Flows*: 'Is the Russian soul still as enigmatic as ever? No, there is no enigma. Was there ever an enigma? What enigma can there be in slavery? But then is this truly a specifically and uniquely Russian law of development? Can it truly be the lot of the Russian soul, and of the Russian soul alone, to evolve not with the growth of freedom but with the growth of slavery? Can this truly be the fate of the Russian soul? . . . It is time for the students and diviners of Russia to understand that the mystique of the Russian soul is simply the result of a thousand years of slavery.'*

---

* Vasily Grossman, *Everything Flows*, trans. Robert and Elizabeth Chandler, with Anna Aslanyan (New York: New York Review of Books, 2009), pp. 179–85.

The modern West and the Moscow ulus of the Golden Horde are separated by a revolution – a special, indeed the most important, revolution in human history: the transition from the hegemony of common, collective consciousness to the pre-eminence of the individual, the private. Human history is split into two manifestly unequal halves. Patriarchal societies have existed for hundreds of generations. People used to identify with the collective, and, like a pack of wolves, depended entirely on the alpha wolf – the chief, khan or tsar. It wasn't until a few centuries ago that a fundamentally different human social order emerged, in which the individual is free. This is what happened in Europe. The 'civilisational revolution' came about a little more easily in the Protestant countries than in the Catholic ones. The Reformation ushered in a new stage of human development, showing that morality could be rooted in something other than fear of the Inquisition, that violence and hypocrisy are not the only way. The West's next step, which Russia also missed out on, was the Enlightenment, whose aim was to teach humans to live a life based on self-determination and reason. The supreme power of God was replaced by *ratio*, reason. Before that famous text beginning with the words 'We, the people' could be conceived of, before life could be shaped in the image of such a constitution, there first had to be a mankind that was conscious of its human dignity.

A 'window to Europe' cannot bridge the huge gap between the two civilisations. Therein lies the tragedy of my homeland:

a small number of my fellow Russians is ready to live in a democracy, but the overwhelming majority still kneels before those in power and tolerates a patriarchal way of life.

The gap between these civilisations is the source of much misunderstanding between Russians and Westerners. Some things that Russians read in Western history books, both great and small, strike them as strange, incomprehensible. For example, Russians wonder why the British dictator Oliver Cromwell would instruct the artist painting his portrait, who apparently 'hadn't noticed' the ugly growths on his face, to paint him 'warts and all'. The king of England might cut off dukes' heads, but a duke would never debase himself before his king, as Russian princes used to do before the tsar, with the words, 'Your slave Vanka [a derogatory diminutive of 'Ivan'] smites the ground with his head.' There, knightly honour; here, princely serfdom. When Winston Churchill and his Conservatives lost the general election in July 1945, it was because the people thought that the nation's hero, the great man who had saved Britain from Hitler, was no longer the right man to lead them in peacetime – yet a Russian could never imagine Stalin leaving his post after winning the war, and going into retirement.

The average Russian doesn't understand the phenomenon of Western lawfulness, just as no one in the West understands Russian lawlessness. The Magna Carta, signed in 1215, includes these two clauses: 'No free man shall be seized or imprisoned, or stripped of his rights or possessions, or outlawed or exiled, or deprived of his standing in any way, nor will we proceed with force against him, or send others to do so, except by the lawful judgment of his equals or by the law of the land'; and 'To no one will we sell, to no one deny or delay right or justice'. These clauses remain enshrined in English law to this day. Yet in thirteenth-century Russia, a relationship of this kind between ruler and subject would have been inconceivable; and it still is.

In the European Middle Ages, the king was still the source of all law; what Magna Carta did was protect the subjects from arbitrary despotism. Then, as long ago as the eighteenth century, the people became the source of all law: in the famous 'Federalist Paper No. 84', Alexander Hamilton, one of the Founding Fathers of the United States, argued against a bill of rights on the grounds that those rights originally belonged to the citizens in their entirety – they had not relinquished them to anyone, and therefore didn't need them to be expressly guaranteed in the constitution: 'The people surrender nothing; and as they retain everything they have no need of particular reservations.' Between this realisation and the Chechen president's demand that Putin be elected Russian president for life lies a bottomless human abyss. The only source of law in the Moscow ulus is, as it always was, the Great Khan. And his serfs simply will not understand or believe that their rights are not granted to them by the state, that human rights are inalienable and independent from the power of a state. Both Russia and its entire population belong, as they always did, to the tsar, and the rights of the individual are subject to arbitrary power.

Now, in the twenty-first century, we are seeing this gap between civilisations widening. Each year, that 'enigmatic' country is becoming more and more 'enigmatic'.

Chapter 7

Hybrid Peace

Our post-war era lasted a long time. Then it turned out that we were living in a pre-war era. And now we are living in wartime.

The dictatorship's one and only goal is to preserve power. Twenty-first-century dictatorships only have one natural enemy: their own people and their 'colourful' revolutions. The TV images that indelibly burnt Hosni Mubarak and Muammar Gaddafi's dismal demise into our memories were like postcards sent by fate to the Kremlin from exotic lands. The hundreds of thousands of people who protested in Moscow in 2012, spoiling the self-proclaimed ruler's inauguration celebrations, signalled approaching danger. The Kremlin's survival instinct set off alarm bells.

The path to the preservation of power leads through war, war as the continuous backdrop to everyday life. A never-ending war is a pill with which regimes can extend their life expectancy. Because this nuclear power, with its arsenal of rusty Soviet-era weapons, could not afford a 'real' war, it started a proxy one instead.

In response to the provocations of the 'colourful revolutions', the regime developed the doctrine of hybrid war. In 2013, Valery Gerasimov, the head of the Russian general staff, published a famous article called 'The Value of Science Is in the Foresight'. In this article, he muses on 'chaos theory' and concludes that, in the modern age, physical military action merely constitutes the end phase of a new style of hybrid warfare, whose aim is to destabilise the situation and create chaos in the enemy state and its society. This goal, he argues, is achieved by means of 'the broad use of political, economic, informational, humanitarian, and other non-military measures – applied in coordination with the protest potential of the population'.* So now the modernised Moscow ulus declared a modernised 'hybrid' war on its enemies. The Cold War is the past; today, we're engaged in something halfway between non-contact and full-contact karate.

Corrupt politicians and journalists, traditional media and social networks disseminating propaganda, cyber-attacks, misinformation, trolling via fake online accounts – all are part of

---

* Valery Gerasimov, 'The Value of Science Is in the Foresight', trans. Robert Coalson, *Military Review* (January–February 2016), 23–9 (p. 24), <https://www.armyupress.army.mil/portals/7/military-review/archives/english/militaryreview_20160228_art008.pdf>.

the Russian general staff's hybrid war. And Europe is already in the thick of it.

The West was wholly unprepared for this war. The politicians' helplessness was painful to witness. The public confusion, inexperience with fake news and manipulated reactions evoked pity and outrage.

The democratic countries totally underestimated Moscow's provocation. In the West, people mentally still lived in the post-war era. They wanted a quiet life, they wanted jobs, gas, peace and no arms to Ukraine. We want things the way they used to be! But the law of survival has changed: when two people have a swordfight and one of them wants peace, they offer their hand and wait for the opponent to shake it. Nowadays, they get their hand lopped off.

The West remains unwilling to cross the red line that marks your willingness to wage war. The khan in Moscow knows this full well, and ruthlessly exploits it. It is difficult for the human psyche to move from a post-war era into a pre-war era, let alone into wartime, and Russia's deployment of 'mass information terrorism' helped it to take that step. Russia is already in a state of war, a semi-declared war against the West. When the coffins of fallen Russian soldiers arrived in Russian cities from Ukraine, they said, 'This is the West's proxy war on Russia.' The coffins helped Russians to complete the mental journey. The war that was happening somewhere in the steppes of the Donbas seemed far away from Westerners' own problems, from London Bridge or the Bataclan in Paris.

They were still labouring under the old illusions of the 1990s. Most western Europeans only heard about the changes taking place in Russia on TV; correspondents reported on democratic reforms, and everyone was naive enough to believe that Russia was evolving into a European nation. Most people in the West didn't understand Russia's social reality, and almost came to see the country as an ally. Western audiences didn't hear the slogans – 'The fight for Russia continues, and we will win', 'We are a victorious people, it's in our genes' – and never saw the smugness, the blatant *schadenfreude* with which Russian TV reported and commented on problems in the West.

The graduates of the Russian KGB academy and military academies have never doubted that the West is pulling the strings of the 'orange' and other coloured revolutions. Washington and Brussels are accused of 'crimes' that they can hardly have perpetrated. In countries that have Facebook and other social networks, mass protests without named leaders or the backing of political parties are a sign of the times. Russia has taken it upon itself to fight revolution all over the world, and from the Kremlin's tower Washington appears as the chief agitator driving those revolutions. State propaganda claims that Western secret services are behind every manifestation of discontent in Russian streets. Moscow believes it has a legitimate interest in making sure that the West condemns rather than fuels protests in Russia and in Russia-friendly dictatorships, from Syria to North Korea. From the point of view of the Moscow ulus, the West declared a hybrid war on the Russian regime on Kyiv's Maidan Square, and it is therefore merely defending itself by launching a hybrid counter-attack.

Western experts and politicians have utterly misread their eastern partner. When Yeltsin nominated Putin as his successor, they made a huge mistake in thinking that they would be dealing with a politician orientated towards the West. In Germany, they allowed themselves to be so beguiled by the German-speaking former KGB officer that Russians who criticised Putin were branded enemies of Russia, while those who defended him were called friends of Russia. Anyone who disapproved of Russia's policies was labelled a 'Russophobe'. How can anyone approve of this hybrid war, which is threatening to spread from my country to the rest of the world like a cancer?

The chief tactic of this new style of warfare is intimidation. The regime wants to scare Western politicians, journalists, diplomats and armed forces into thinking that Russia is prepared for military conflict with NATO and, if necessary, a Third World War. The military provocations along NATO's eastern borders are designed to demonstrate Russia's sinister willingness to take risks. This daring and dangerous all-or-nothing gamble, which could end up wiping humanity from the face of the earth, is a test of nerves that can surely end only one way. The West will never want to engage in nuclear war. The Kremlin knows that Western countries are reluctant to sacrifice people's lives for Donetsk, the Russian-speaking industrial metropolis in eastern Ukraine, and no matter how long this fatal poker game goes on for, the democratic countries will keep giving in and be forced to swallow whatever the Moscow ulus throws at them. We have already seen it with the wars in Chechnya, Georgia and Ukraine. The West will always pull back, be it in Ukraine, in the Caucasus, possibly even in the Baltic – and who knows where next. It won't risk entering into a Final World War over Mariupol or Narva. In this game of blackmail, Western democracies don't stand a chance.

The Kremlin's strategists think like common gangsters. Back in the day, they engaged in gang warfare until they had control of St Petersburg; then they won the gang wars that spread from St Petersburg to the rest of this vast country, and took control of the state; now they are attacking other states, and committing crimes all over the world with impunity. The Dutch families who lost relatives in the skies over the Russian-Ukrainian border were perhaps the first Europeans to realise that a hybrid war is also a war. Fear is a weapon. Fear paralyses its victim. At the KGB academy, students were taught how to exploit fear.

The world was content to fire hundreds of Tomahawk missiles at Assad's regime, which was killing its own people with sarin gas; but it handles North Korea's Kim Jong-un with kid gloves, no doubt because of his thermonuclear warheads. The Kremlin has taken notice, and the news is good: it suggests that, in the nuclear power game, you can keep doubling your stakes. According to the unwritten law of survival seen in Russian prisons, it is not the stronger who wins but whoever is prepared to see things through to the end. And now the rest of the world is compelled to live by it too.

Predictably, NATO's troops have moved eastwards in response to the provocations along the border. Defence budgets are growing, and NATO is considering further expansion by admitting Finland and Sweden. News such as this is instantly interpreted by the Russian propaganda machine as examples of Western aggression. The West simply isn't ready for this new war, and reacts as in the 'good' old days, when the rules of the game were clear and it still mattered whether or not your tank divisions and missiles outnumbered your enemy's. They are gambling with a cheat and trying to make him see reason, but he has no intention of playing by the rules. He knows that his opponents can't leave the table and will endlessly keep trying to talk him round. The game will continue being played according to his rules. There is compassionate talk of the cheat wanting to be treated as an 'equal', but all he does with that 'equality' is set his own rules and use his veto to torpedo all international efforts to preserve democracy.

The team captain is no longer interested in the opinion of his 'partners'. After the death of Alexander Litvinenko (the former secret service agent who, among other things, investigated the 1999 bomb attacks on residential buildings and published the book *Blowing Up Russia: Terror from Within*, and who was poisoned by the FSB in London in 2006), the Kremlin concluded that any crime will go unpunished. Why should it care a jot for public opinion in the West, given the laissez-faire response to the 2008 assault on Georgia, the annexation of Crimea and the invasion of Ukraine?

It seems paradoxical that the latest Western technology, which could only be developed thanks to democracy and by people who were free, is being deployed to undermine that same democracy. But Western technology always was the one thing that the Moscow ulus wanted from the West for its war against the West. Think of Peter the Great. In the Information Age, what it wants is IT weapons.

Freedom of expression, democracy's greatest achievement, is ruthlessly abused. Russian state media representatives are regarded as journalists and treated accordingly, but the West has again misunderstood the situation. These people have nothing to do with journalism. Information warriors who do everything in their power to incite the Russian people against the West are not journalists. The democratic countries are still failing to see this, and decry any measures taken against Russia's TV combat troops as curtailing freedom of speech. Real journalists, however, wouldn't broadcast fake news of the rape of a Russian girl by 'Muslim refugees' in Berlin with the sole aim of inciting outrage and angry protests. That's how hybrid war works – it can invade any home, anywhere in the world.

We can see how efficient the Russian secret services are in their use of social networks to create an atmosphere of intolerance and hate. The 'opinion factories' are working away day and night. An army of trolls is sending shitstorms and persecution campaigns around the world and leaving thousands of hate-filled comments online. These days, society's mood is set by cyberspace, and hundreds of thousands of fake accounts are affecting our atmosphere. When it comes to troublemaking trolls, no expense is spared.

In the West, too, there are many journalists, politicians, businesspeople and bloggers who fancy making some extra cash, and who accept payment in exchange for writing 'pro-Russian' articles, filming reports, organising conferences and seminars, and posting comments online. Why should 'little people' do without their little bit of money, if 'big people' don't shy away from accepting a job from the Russian fuel pump? When someone like Gerhard Schröder, the former head of a democratic state, unabashedly takes up such a post – why should his fellow citizens feel embarrassed about working for his employer too, on the side? After all, everyone has mouths to feed.

Schröder's venality has had a lasting impact on the Great Khan's view of the West: what lies behind the democratic facade, then, if democratic leaders behave that way? Once again, heads of government are travelling to Sarai to pay homage and placate.

Moscow's corrupt system is producing metastases that are spreading throughout the world, audaciously and ruthlessly corrupting parts of the elite. Russian money is eating away at the West. In the last two decades, billions in dirty cash has been transferred into Western bank accounts, and the moment that bank staff and bureaucrats became willing to turn a blind eye to the money's criminal origins, democratic values started to corrode. What good is a democracy, if it doesn't distinguish between honest and dishonest income?

As an interpreter, I have frequently witnessed the solemnity with which Switzerland has welcomed Russian criminal capital. When I first arrived here, I expected Switzerland to be a place where money didn't stink. But then I realised that money merely stinks differently in different countries. In Russia, there is no mistaking its smell: low wages reek of sweat, misery and hopelessness, but big money hums with deceit, crime, fraud, bribery and contempt. In Russia, it is by definition impossible for big money to be clean. Every Russian knows it. In Switzerland, meanwhile, the mechanism euphemistically called 'money laundering' works perfectly: the banks pay taxes, and the state funnels those taxes to bureaucrats, schools, farmers, authors, and so on, and dirty money becomes clean.

Where does 'unclean' money end and 'clean' money begin? My interpreter's salary, paid directly by a nouveau riche Muscovite, was doubtless still 'unclean'. The administrative fees of the private banks in Zurich's Bahnhofstrasse were too, I think, though the bankers probably wouldn't agree. Is this money – a source of income for the Swiss state – now clean, or not quite clean? How do you distinguish between honest and dishonest work? Can the Swiss banking system possibly be honest, with all that dirty, dishonestly acquired cash? After all, the country doesn't live off its cows and their milk – on the contrary, the only reason it still has cows and farmers is that they get subsidies from the state, which in turn gets its money from the banks.

Dirty Russian money buys Western villas, yachts, football

clubs, journalists, bureaucrats, politicians, opinions and decisions. Russia has systematised the export of corruption, and by
tying in entrepreneurs, businesspeople, politicians and experts,
the *ulus* is lobbying on its own behalf. The West gratefully
submits to this 'cash assault', a crucial manoeuvre in hybrid
warfare. We all have mouths to feed.

The Moscow regime doesn't care a fig whether its money
shores up left-wing or right-wing parties in western Europe; it
backs whichever political factions want to weaken the democratic system and destabilise politics. No wonder that both
left-wing and right-wing extremists are among the most vocal
European defenders of Russian 'sharp-elbow politics' and the
annexation of Crimea. The species of the 'useful idiot' discovered by Lenin back in the day is proliferating and taking
over new habitats. Lenin is supposed to have said once that
'the capitalists will sell us the rope with which we will hang
them' – today, they are buying the capitalists as well as their
rope. There was a time when sympathising with Moscow was
a matter of ideological conviction, but the current Russian
regime represents no ideology of any kind that could reasonably
be palatable to 'right-left' extremists. The KGB's relationship
with its agents in the West never was founded on ideology
alone, and now, too, the work done by the Russian secret service
is rooted in pragmatism.

One of the chief aims of this hybrid war is to fragment
the West, to play the European countries off each other. The
Kremlin's hackers are penetrating the computers of Western

politicians and infecting entire networks with viruses – but while computer networks can be fixed fairly quickly, other kinds of infection are harder to cure. The world has caught the virus of general mistrust: two elections ago, it was only marginal voters who opted for Marine Le Pen's party; now, it is the second-biggest party in France. Infusions of Russian money have no doubt done Front National a lot of good, and who knows, maybe the party will come out on top in the next elections. German right-wing extremists, too, have become politically acceptable, and now represent the Moscow ulus's interests in the Bundestag. All over Europe, the right-wing populist parties that are attacking democratic values are being instrumentalised by Moscow for its hybrid war. As Europe threatens to suffocate in political correctness, there is a growing enthusiasm for a strongman in the Kremlin. Russian propaganda is awakening instincts normally suppressed by civilisation, and European voters, unsettled by the migrants coming over from Muslim countries, are yearning for a firm hand.

The rapid ascent of the German right-wing party Alternative für Deutschland was made possible only by the votes of hundreds of thousands of Russian immigrants. For the Soviet secret services, working with émigrés was always much easier than recruiting 'actual natives' in the West who had never known Russian fear – former Soviet citizens are more receptive to blackmail and other forms of psychological influence. In Germany, this influence is exerted not only directly, by Russian TV and social networks, but also via the various cultural and educational organisations financed by the Russkiy Mir Foundation in Moscow. Such organisations are created and run by the Russian secret services for propaganda purposes; the result of all this is that tens of thousands of Russians take to the streets in German cities chanting racist slogans, and the AfD sits in the German parliament. The enemies of the European community are on the march.

Donald Trump – whose election victory was toasted with champagne in the Duma – fell out with Europe because he questioned the value of NATO. Any friction among the members of the transatlantic alliance constitutes a victory in Russia's war against the West. The far-right eastern European elites that are in power in Hungary and Poland positively radiate xenophobia. The West is divided – and for the Great Khan in Moscow, that's a victory. His allies are all those who question democratic values, the rights and freedoms of the individual, openness and compassion, and his undisguised aim is the collapse of Europe, which Russian TV summons and solicits, night after night.

The regime in Moscow is giving the civilised world a masterclass in the ability of dictatorships to defy the twenty-first century. When the president of the world's most powerful democracy said that Assad must go, that a dictator could not be allowed to poison children and women with chemical weapons, the Great Khan replied, no, Assad will stay. We all know what happened then: Obama retired, and Assad is still in power.

The hybrid war is a zero-waste production. Even refugees

from regions where Russian fighter jets once bombed those who opposed Assad are deployed as weapons to destabilise European democracies. The European dream of a mobile world without borders has turned into a world filled with refugees, and twenty-first-century Europeans busy campaigning for the environment and animal rights suddenly spot a camp of refugees from the blood-soaked Middle Ages right under their window. Troll troops and an army of every thinkable and unthinkable type of 'useful idiot' are stoking the refugee crisis, using all means at their disposal. The Russian general staff has succeeded brilliantly in its task of creating social tension and destabilising domestic politics in Europe.

The bait used to catch Western politicians is that, in the war on terror, Russia must at all costs be won over as an ally. The Islamist wave of terror in Europe is ruthlessly exploited by Russian propaganda. Anytime there is a terrorist attack in the West, the Russian Foreign Office sends a message of condolence formulated to suggest that such loss of life could be avoided, if only Washington, Brussels, London, Paris, Berlin, or wherever the tragedy happened, was willing to work with Russia – or, to put it more simply: 'If you misbehave, you'll keep getting punched in the face.' The 2013 Boston Marathon bombing demonstrated the extent to which the ulus exploits Islamist terrorists for its own benefit: Tamerlan Tsarnaev spent several months in Russia in 2012, including visits to Dagestan and Chechnya under the FSB's tactful supervision. He met with underground Islamist fighters, some of whom were liquidated shortly afterwards.

Tsarnaev returned to Moscow safe and sound, and then went to the US to carry out the bomb attack. His FSB mentors could be proud of him and his brother Dzhokhar.

The West is losing the hybrid war. Politicians and businessmen are prepared to betray Ukraine for their 'economic interests', and the more barefaced the actions in this hybrid war, the greater the increase in Russian–German trade turnover (22.8 per cent in 2017). In 1980, sixty-five countries boycotted the Moscow Olympics following the Russian invasion of Afghanistan; now, the reborn empire has invaded a sovereign state in Europe, annexed a large part of it and is conducting a war that has cost 10,000 lives so far – but not a single country saw fit to boycott the FIFA World Cup in Russia.

The Moscow ulus has won because its propaganda machine has scattered toxic seeds of doubt over fundamental human values. It has won because there is a tangible sense of disappointment in democracy among people. Large sections of the population are ready to sacrifice their freedom for the war on terror. They are scared – and that was the point. Now the citizens of a country that is proud of its freedom are happy to have their phone calls listened to without the need for a warrant, and for their bank details and account statements, their IDs and medical history to be freely accessible. The war on terror leads to complete control, to a police state.

The conflict between the new Moscow ulus and the West is also being staged in the post-Soviet realm, where old scores remain to be settled. NATO's eastwards expansion happened because Poland, Chechnya, Hungary, Lithuania, Latvia and Estonia wanted it to. If the alliance's permanent representatives had rejected these states, their own citizens would have been nonplussed. What prompted this historical decision was not NATO, but the tough experiences these countries have made in the past.

Moscow still doesn't take the former Soviet republics' independence seriously, which is why the new nation states hate and fear their former big brother. Countries with a large percentage of Russians among their population are afraid of being mutilated like Ukraine. The secret services have vividly shown how saving Russians from the 'threat of genocide' is done, and the country might at any moment consider itself 'forced' to invade, in order to 'protect the lives of Russian-speaking minorities'.

The nations at the edges of the empire exploited a window of opportunity created by the chaos and the power vacuum that followed perestroika to rid themselves of the Russian occupier. The window was open only briefly before the prison of nations was resurrected, and the governments of the new states quickly had to find a way to secure their continued independence. They looked for a powerful ally, and found NATO. The former Russian colonies hurried to join the alliance, and the young sovereign states extended an invitation to NATO – a survival strategy that, for example in the Baltics, turned out to be fully justified. They were watching Russia's democratic development with suspicion, and wanted to avoid 'little green men' fighting Baltic 'fascists' for the rights of Russians in Riga or

Narva. Ukraine lacked the same powerful ally, and was attacked and torn apart. Can there be a more convincing argument for NATO's eastwards expansion?

In reality, then, it was not a case of NATO pushing eastwards, but of the eastern European nations pushing westwards, away from the Moscow ulus. When the Baltic republics were saved by the Western alliance, the Kremlin was outraged and claimed that US and German politicians had broken the promise they made in 1990 that NATO would not expand beyond the Oder–Neisse line. It was yet another attempt by the Sarai propaganda machine to twist the facts. The Kremlin quoted the then US secretary of state, James Baker, as saying that NATO would not move 'one inch to the east', but he was clearly referring to East German territory in the context of the Soviet army's withdrawal. The main protagonists in that story, Baker and George H. W. Bush, claimed emphatically that the subject of NATO expansion never came up during negotiations over German reunification, and no such promise could therefore have been made. As the German historian Heinrich August Winkler has said, 'Recent claims – oft-repeated, including by Putin – that NATO has broken its promise not to expand eastwards are an old myth.' NATO's eastward expansion did not cause the hybrid war against the West – it was just another excuse.

People in the West are scared of unambiguous words. It is not merely a question of political correctness. They don't want to talk about the war, even though the war is already in full swing. They are scared of self-fulfilling prophecies, of harbingers of doom, and naively think that if you don't talk about the war it will simply pass like a summer storm. But running away from words has never yet saved anyone from their meaning.

If the West had reacted quickly and adequately to the bombardment of Chechnya and the attack on Georgia, Crimea may never have been occupied, and there may never have been war in Donbas or the mass executions carried out by the Russian-backed Syrian dictator. Impunity emboldens.

The half-baked Western sanctions on Russia express the tentative hope that economic problems might create discontent among Russians, and inspire them to protest against their regime. Sadly, it is a vain hope. There's a famous Russian saying: 'Beat your own people, so that others will fear you.' It is inconceivable that London or Berlin would suddenly ban all food imports – if they did, the country would be rocked by an explosive uprising the very same day. When Russia issued such an edict, however, it only increased people's already overabundant support for the ruler. The Great Khan knows only too well that the democratic European governments differ from his own: democracies have a duty to take care of their people and their future, but in a dictatorship there is only the duty to obey.

People in the West, panicked by the prospect of economic chaos and war, are more likely to elect new governments and replace opponents of Putin with Putin sympathisers, than that economic collapse and rising food prices will inspire the Russian people to rise up against the state. In fact, this seems to be happening already. European governments are at odds with each other over the question of sanctions; and they will never implement real sanctions (stopping gas and oil imports, banning Russia from SWIFT, trade embargoes), because the pro-Russian lobby will always block any such measures.

The conflict between Russia and the West is still far from resolved – it has not even reached its climax. Nevertheless, the hybrid war waged by the Moscow ulus could prove an opportunity for Europe. Working out a common defence strategy in the face of this new challenge may give fresh impetus to the European community and reinvigorate its faded sense of unity. Such a crisis, danger or threat might compel Europe to define itself anew, to rediscover what it consists of, where it begins and ends, and what it stands for. As war looms, Europe has a chance to see itself as a coherent entity again. In the twenty-first century, there is no such thing as a distant, localised war any more. Every war is now a European one. And this European war has already started.

Chapter 8

Two Russian Peoples

On a searing hot afternoon, a Russian-Swiss border sprang up in the Valley of the Kings in Egypt. The paths of a group of Swiss tourists and a group of Russian tourists had crossed in the tomb of Pharaoh Ramses IX. Photography was forbidden. Flashing cameras announced the Russians' arrival. The law-abiding Swiss, outraged and deeply wounded, hissed. One briefly left his girlfriend by the entrance, approached a guard and told him, in English, that people were taking photos in the tomb. The guard, weary from the heat, picked himself up and blew his whistle. He ran inside, and the Swiss followed him and pointed out the offenders. Two police officers came running. A little while later, the Swiss man returned to his girlfriend, exhilarated. The girl looked at him, her eyes full of pride and love.

Two mentalities clashed here. You couldn't imagine a young man in Russia proudly telling his girlfriend that he's ratted someone out to the cops. The code of honour that prevails here, and which originated in prison culture, strictly forbids it. She would no longer love him.

People report other people everywhere, of course, but Swiss denunciations are not the same as Russian ones. A Swiss citizen will report someone out of a feeling of solidarity with a state that is seen as protecting its citizens from crime and other dangers. A Russian citizen will report someone because they are scared of their own state. In Switzerland, the relationship between an individual and the state differs fundamentally from that in Russia, where the state is, and always has been, a foreign occupying power from which people have to protect themselves.

You'd have thought that thirty years of free exchange of ideas, goods, people and financial laundry would have contributed to a general diffusion of values. No matter where you go, be it Zurich, Berlin or Moscow, you see the same cars, the same fashions, the same ads, the same IKEAs. But appearances are deceptive. Globalisation has failed to bridge the gulf between Russian and Western minds. Open borders don't mean that people can afford to travel abroad. The Iron Curtain has been replaced by a Golden Curtain, and even nowadays, two-thirds of Russians don't have a passport and three-quarters have never left the territory of the former USSR. This makes you think, especially in light of Alexander von Humboldt's comment that 'the most dangerous world views are those of people who have never seen the world'. Most Russians have no conception of democracy, because they have never lived in a democracy or had a chance to learn about it. The reforms of the 1990s gave democratic principles a bad reputation. In Russia, 'democracy' has connotations of chaos, breakdown, empty promises and demagoguery. They don't understand that a democratic state is a stable system based on power-sharing and free competition between political parties. People think that an authoritarian system is a natural and fitting form of power. They want stability, not upheaval. Chulpan Khamatova, a popular actor and founder of the charitable child cancer foundation The Gift of Life, summed it up thus: 'Given the choice between revolution and the kind of life they live in North Korea, I would choose North Korea.'

Russians love strong tsars, not weak ones. They idolise tyrants and loathe those who seek to moderate tyranny; that's how it was with Ivan the Terrible and Boris Godunov, with Stalin and Gorbachev – not because that age-old cliché regarding the Russians is true, but because they learnt their lesson from centuries spent fighting for survival. In Russia, the alternative to dictatorship is not democracy, the alternative to oppression is not freedom: rather, the alternatives are dictatorship or anarchy, order or chaos. I remember reading a famous fable in primary school, in which an oak tree and a reed argue about who is stronger and more resilient: 'Every breath of wind moves you to and fro,' says the oak dismissively. The reed doesn't reply.

A little later, a violent storm draws in. The oak pushes against the storm and buckles, but the reed gives in to the gusts and survives unscathed. If you bend, you don't break. For us, they were nothing but words, but I now imagine that, for our old teacher, they represented her personal experience of surviving in twentieth-century Russia.

Western observers had long remarked on the Russians' fatalism and infinite forbearance, including the French diplomat Maurice Paléologue (1859–1944), who wrote: 'One of the moral characteristics I am always noticing in the Russians is the readiness with which they accept defeat, and the resigned way in which they bow before the blows of fortune. Often enough they do not even wait for the decrees of fate to be pronounced, but submit and adapt themselves accordingly, by anticipation so to speak.'* The submissiveness with which Russians endure their pitiful condition and oppression by the state, and which seems so strange to Western travellers, is the key component of the Russian survival strategy. If you bend, you don't break.

Fear is a wellspring of life, and it comes as naturally as breathing and eating. It is part of our instinct for self-preservation. Anyone who sacrifices themselves for their principles is trying to defy nature. For the majority, it doesn't matter under whose flag the next Mongol attack arrives – they

---

* Maurice Paléologue, *An Ambassador's Memoirs*, trans. F. A. Holt, vol. 2 (New York: George H. Doran Co, 1925), p. 112 (30 November 1915).

will adapt to any dictatorship. If their ancestors had not adapted to Batu Khan and to People's Commissar Dzerzhinsky, they would have survived neither the Tartars nor the communists.

I was named after my grandfather, Mikhail Shishkin, who was arrested in 1930, during the Soviet Union's collectivisation period. At the time, he was living with his wife and two sons, aged nine and four (the four-year-old, Pavel, would become my father) in a village in the region of Tambov. The other peasants said nothing, but he protested: 'Why are you taking away our only cow? How am I meant to feed my two children?' He was taken into custody, and my grandma never saw her Misha again. He later died in a Siberian prison camp.

In her final years, Grandma started getting confused. She would say things that made no sense, and lost her sense of time. Then her eyesight failed, and she spent her last years living in a small room in the home of her son, my father, where she would sit in the dark for days on end. I called her whenever I could, and would yell into the phone so that she could hear me better: 'Babushka, hi, it's me, Misha!'

'Misha?' she would ask, startled. 'Who is this? Misha?'

She was probably reliving that day over and over, each time thinking anew that they were about to arrest her husband. She yelled into the phone: 'Misha! Where are they taking you? – Please don't! Let him go! What are you doing?'

I tried to interrupt her. 'Babushka, calm down, it's me, your Misha!'

But she wasn't listening. She kept yelling, trying to get her

Misha away from them, trying to save him: 'Let him go! What did we ever do to you? Let him go! Misha! Misha!'

Back then, the people who said nothing survived. That's how natural selection works in Russia.

Russian history has shown that, generation after generation, the state would eliminate or drive into exile anyone who didn't fit in with the system. The others learnt the Russian art of survival. If you tried to raise your head you would be decapitated, so it was better for your health to say nothing and lick the boots of those in power.

This is how the chief of police in Gogol's *Dead Souls* describes the interaction between the people and the state: 'The chief of police observed that there was no need to be afraid of a mutiny, that there was a rural captain of police to see to it that it did not occur, and that even if the rural captain of police did not go there himself but sent his cap, the sight of his cap alone would be sufficient to drive the peasants to their new places of residence.'* Like Gessler's hat in the legend of William Tell, the police captain's headgear symbolises state authority. And the Russian peasants had more than enough reason to tremble before the captain's cap, just as the captain himself knew exactly why he trembled before the major's cap, and on it goes, up the social ladder, until, trembling, you get to the Monomakh's Cap. The actual, physical person plays no role in all that trembling.

---

* Nikolai Gogol, *Dead Souls*, trans. David Magarshack (London: Penguin, 1961), p. 165.

It is the superior rank itself that instils fear. And those at the very top in turn tremble before those who tremble before them.

The source of Russian state power and of all law is violence, pure and simple. The state can do what it wants with us. The people are at the mercy of an occupying power. As Nadezhda Mandelstam, the widow of the murdered poet Osip Mandelstam, once described it, 'It's as if we were living on a sated ogre's kitchen shelf.'

The state is your destiny. Mere mortals cannot influence the system, in the same way that you can't choose your destiny. That is why the state is sacred, and why the tsar, who symbolises the state, is a sacred figure.

As the famous saying goes, 'The tsar is good – it's the boyars who are evil.' Indeed, that is how the 'separation of powers' works in Russia: good things happen thanks to the good tsar, bad things happen because of those evil boyars (the powerful men who surround him). It has been an effective tactic in Russia for centuries. During Stalin's purges, millions sent letters to the Kremlin, saying, 'If only Stalin knew!' It is a country of evil boyars, and only the tsar can sort them out (people thought that the secret services had arrested their husband, father, sister or son by mistake, and that Stalin knew nothing about it). Since 2001, there's been an annual programme on Russian TV called *Direct Line with Vladimir Putin*, where hundreds of thousands of people submit complaints and petitions concerning injustices they have suffered at the hands of corrupt officials and the like. For many, this 'direct line' to the tsar is their last chance of getting their pension paid out, or getting running water supplied to their remote village. One especially popular video appeal to the president (which you can watch on YouTube) featured people who had been cheated out of their life savings, which they'd invested in a new residential development. In a provincial city somewhere, well-dressed women and men knelt in front of a memorial to fallen soldiers, begging 'dear Vladimir Vladimirovich' to recover their money from the developer. This uniquely Russian form of kneeling protest was remarked on by Mikhail Saltykov-Shchedrin in his novel *The History of a Town* (1870): 'And the Glupovites knelt and waited. They knew they were in revolt, but they could not help kneeling.'*

Another uniquely Russian form of protest is the worshipping of brutal dictators of the past. I remember well how, back in Soviet times, in the 1970s, you often saw little pictures of Stalin behind lorry drivers' windscreens. Stalin did not symbolise mass murder, but a just order, which the ordinary people missed during the later years of the utterly corrupt Soviet Union. In a country of slaves, people craved fairness. Inside the barracks, they wanted everyone to be equal.

This form of protest is becoming increasingly common in Russia these days. For the *Name of Russia* project, broadcast by the state-owned TV channel Rossiya-1, people were asked

---

* M. E. Saltykov-Shchedrin, *The History of a Town*, trans. I. P. Foote (London: Head of Zeus, 2016), p. 99.

to vote for their favourite historical figure. Stalin was leading by a big margin, but before the third and decisive round the voting was nullified and restarted, and the head of the channel eventually crowned the prince and saint Alexander Nevsky the greatest Russian in history. Political correctness, Russian-style. The fact that the cult of Stalin is so popular reveals a lot about what is going on in the country: Stalin represents the war on corruption, social injustice, the ostentatious wealth of the elites, and the poverty and hopelessness experienced by millions of people; and when they say that Stalin was the best ruler Russia ever had, they are expressing their conviction that only a strongman can establish a just order in Russia. This sends a clear signal to the Kremlin. When it comes to their subjects, Moscow's khans have been bloody lucky.

In *Anna Karenina*, Levin asks a peasant, 'Have you heard about the war, Mihalich? . . . What do you think now? Ought we to fight for the Christians?' 'Why should we bother our heads? Alexander Nikolayevich our Emperor has thought about it for us, as he always does. He knows best. . . .'*

'Why should we bother our heads?' You aren't supposed to think, be it about war or whether they will tarmac your street. What you are supposed to do is submit and do as you're told. Everyone knows that showing initiative is undesirable, and that everything, good or bad, comes from above. Most Russians,

---

* Leo Tolstoy, *Anna Karenina*, trans. Rosemary Edmonds (Harmondsworth: Penguin, 1954), p. 842.

particularly in the provinces, still believe that they can't live without support from the state, and expect to be provided for, to have free medical care and social services. They think that they can't achieve anything by themselves, that the state will take care of everything. This is how soldiers, inmates in prisons and children in classrooms are 'looked after': whatever you do, don't take the initiative – we'll take care of everything. This doesn't sound much like an emerging civil society. It is the behaviour of serfs, who look up from below, who are used to arbitrary power and place their free will in the hands of those who wield it. There is a deeply ingrained sense that nothing depends on you, that you can't make any decisions. You can't blame them for it; the experience of generations shows that if you take the initiative you will be punished. To survive, you must remain passive and never show initiative – it is one of the golden rules of the Russian mentality.

Creativity requires freedom. In Russia, being gifted, having a creative mind, hinders rather than helps if you want to rise through professional or social ranks. Fields that call for creative freedom, such as scientific and other research, consequently yield only meagre fruit. When Ivan Turgenev visited the Exposition Universelle in Paris in 1867, he noted with chagrin how little Russia contributed to mankind's technological advancement. Nowadays, in the twenty-first century, Russians are perhaps just as irked when they see how backward the country is in almost all areas of technology. Modern Russia produces no advanced technology itself; instead, it makes use of

Western developments. All those everyday things used by the Russian 'elite' – computers, gadgets, cars, clothes – are either produced in the West or based on Western designs. Everything that humanity has achieved is grounded in the most essential democratic value of all: individual freedom.

Soviet propaganda kept praising the achievements of Soviet science like a mantra. What they never mentioned was that the industrialisation of the 1920s and 1930s was made possible by US firms setting up industrial enterprises in the Soviet Union, capable of managing the complete technological manufacturing cycle, fully installed and ready to start production. During the Second World War, Russia relied on technology provided by the US Lend-Lease programme. After the war, entire facilities were moved from occupied Germany to the Soviet Union. They 'took over' not only its technology and equipment, but engineers, specialists and scientists. One example of this is the development of the Soviet Union's most famous export, a weapon that has conquered the world market unlike anything else manufactured in Russia. Its presumed inventor was Mikhail Kalashnikov, and about a hundred million of these rifles have been produced to date. When the famous German weapons manufacturer Hugo Schmeisser and his colleagues were forcibly moved to the Soviet Union in 1946, they were taken by special train to Izhevsk, where they lived and worked under strict supervision for several years. Schmeisser's activities there are still shrouded in secrecy – but Izhevsk is where the Kalashnikov assault rifle was produced.

Without the secret formulas that the Soviet secret services extracted from the US, the scientists working under executioner-in-chief Lavrentiy Beria (whom Stalin had tasked with building a Soviet atom bomb) would have taken far longer to develop Russian nuclear weapons. In his novel *The First Circle*, Solzhenitsyn describes what it was like for inventors and researchers working in the *sharashka* (a prison camp for scientists and engineers). Among them was the man to whom the Soviet Union owed its proudest achievement – the conquest of space – and whose name remained taboo until his death. Sergei Korolev, the father of the Soviet space programme, spent six years in the Gulag. He had been accused of planning to assassinate Stalin using technology he had developed himself, and, after being tortured and having his family threatened, signed a confession in which he was forced to declare his involvement in a supposedly counter-revolutionary plot. In the camp on the banks of the Kolyma, where he nearly starved to death, they knocked out his teeth and broke his jaw, and he fell ill with scurvy. He was then sent to a *sharashka* to build engines, which saved his life. After the Second World War, he rose to become chief designer for the Soviet space programme, and in 1945 was ordered to go to Berlin to study German rockets, and to unearth any former colleagues of Wernher von Braun who were still living in Germany. He returned to the Soviet Union with German rocket designs and German rocket-builders. In Russia, Braun's former assistants and colleagues were involved in designing Soviet rockets, and the rocket types they developed back then are still in use today. The national space and lunar programme, however, limped along only slowly, and work on the N1 moon rocket ceased in 1974 without anything to show for it. In the end, the Soviet Union lost the race with the West. Its outdated technology and production backlogs ultimately resulted in perestroika and the fall of the Soviet Union.

In a way, the new Russia has itself become a *sharashka*. The regime's serfs have no control over their own lives. Today you have a small business; tomorrow someone in a uniform with epaulettes takes it from you and gives it to their nephew. Today you own a flat in Moscow; tomorrow there's a 'clean-up' and you're 'voluntarily' rehoused. When you woke up this morning you were the omnipotent mayor of a Russian metropolis; tomorrow you'll wake up a refugee. Today you're an oligarch or minister for economic development; tomorrow you'll be lying on a cot in your cell, one prisoner among many. If you can't make plans for your own future, you live in the present. The general motto is 'After me the flood'. Everyone is in a hurry to enjoy the feast today, for tomorrow might already be too late. As the Russian proverb has it, 'No one's safe from the beggar's staff or jail'; and so the boyars live the high life in their palaces, the rank and file are getting drunk in their shacks, and no one ever saves anything for the future. You celebrate this day, because the next an evil fairy godmother who outranks you could turn your carriage into a pumpkin.

If you want to achieve anything, you need to join the social food chain. If you want to climb the ladder, mediocrity and a willingness to do anything for your boss are the prerequisites for success. In recent years millions of functionaries have cropped up in the new Russia, who do nothing except allow themselves to be bribed. They are willing to break any and all moral laws for the right to remain in this food chain. Everything in Russia's political system is rotten, because the system spoils everything, from the top down. Our decay, that of the people at the bottom, is feeding the decay at the top, and those at the top are feeding the decay below; and so we come full circle. The whole country is afflicted with rot.

Basically, not only is the state not bound by any laws, there is no state at all. All we see is a mock version erected for the benefit of the Western observer. In reality, Russia has a mafia-like power structure that exploits the state machinery. As the Soviet prosecutor said at the Nuremberg trials, 'These criminals seized power, and made the state the instrument of their criminal actions.' Exactly the same is happening in Russia today.

In the Russian political system, everything is a fiction: the division of powers, legislature, self-governance – all of it. Or take independent courts: you cannot win a trial without bribing the judge. Important trials are decided 'from above', and courts exist to put people who protest against this corrupt system behind bars. The judiciary has become nothing more than a prison authority. All that remains of the courts is a shell, like the dummy planes people set up at airfields during the Second World War to deceive the enemy. The machines looked real, but they couldn't fly. In the same way, the written laws and regulations are dummy laws and regulations. There is only one unwritten law that works perfectly: the law of power, which everyone infallibly obeys – because if you don't, it might cost you your life.

Imagine, for instance, that you're out and about with your son, who is sleeping peacefully in his pushchair, and come to a busy road. The written law is clear on this point. Pushchairs are weaker than speeding SUVs, and the purpose of a legal system is to protect the weak from the strong. To protect little humans in pushchairs, roads have zebra crossings, where the SUV is meant to stop for you. I have no doubt that those among you who have ever walked the streets of a Russian city will have come across a scene that sent shivers down your spine. Russian cities have zebra crossings too, and no one can deny that SUVs are stronger than pushchairs – which is why, in Russia, SUVs have priority. You'd be the last person not to stick to the rules and give way to the oncoming SUV. If you were to insist that, legally, you have priority, the SUV would run you and your pushchair over, and it would be your fault. You, and not the driver of the SUV, would have broken the one and only law that counts.

The vertical of power has its own rigid rules. You are strictly forbidden to accept bribes that are above your pay grade, as Gogol's police superintendent, hand outstretched, explains to his subordinates in *The Government Inspector*. Pocketing a bribe without sharing it with your superiors is an unpardonable crime. And the worst thing you can be is honest and incorruptible. The hierarchy won't tolerate it.

A life spent not breaking unwritten laws inevitably means breaking written ones. No one follows the latter, least of all the public bodies responsible for legal protections and making sure that laws and regulations are followed. This is the 'Russian paradox': everyone is essentially a criminal, because everyone obeys the unwritten laws and therefore breaks the written ones. Every Russian has one foot in jail. Then, too, there's the fact that for so many years, so many people who weren't common criminals, thieves or murderers were sent to the camps, for ideological and political reasons. This explains people's strange attitude, so often remarked on in Russian literature, towards those who are caught and sent to prison: prisoners are not seen as criminals or lawbreakers – they are mainly thought of as unlucky. Everyone breaks the law, and it's pure chance whether or not you are caught; this one was unlucky, that one ill-fated. They lock this one up today, that one tomorrow, and the day after that it'll be you lying on your bunk in a cell, despite not having actually committed a crime.

The 'vertical of power' is a clan hierarchy. The new regime's next generation is already occupying all the leading positions in the country. The social ladder is the same as it was in the Middle Ages. There's a popular joke in Russia: the son of a colonel can't become a general, because the general also has a son. A new hereditary state aristocracy has emerged: higher-ranking Russian officials exclusively produce gifted children, who, after graduating from nursery school, become executives and directors at the leading state banks and state corporations.

Nevertheless, even these wunderkinder can't be certain that what they inherit really belongs to them. In Russia, the free market is regarded as a system of state property, where what you have depends entirely on 'administrative resources' and loyalty. If the head of the clan falls from grace, their retinue plunges into poverty with them.

Meanwhile, at the bottom of the food chain, the silent people are vegetating away. Farmers, workers, doctors and teachers stay silent and watch TV. They flee into a parallel televised world where, for a few hours, you can forget the misery, degradation, poverty, inequality and lack of prospects, the dire state of the country's education system and the woeful medical care that you can't afford. Alcohol, that well-tried Russian remedy, is even better at solving all those unsolvable problems.

Occasionally, when there is an 'election', the state needs the silent masses to speak. A cohort of extras is recruited to help organise the spectacle. Teachers, for example, are duty-bound to help out at polling stations in tens of thousands of schools all over the country, and thus play an active part in electoral fraud: being educated people, they are responsible for the 'accurate' counting of votes cast. Anyone who refuses is likely to quickly lose their job. As I said, everyone has mouths to feed.

Russia doesn't have the sort of mafia you find in other countries, which operates in parallel with governments. The Russian Cosa Nostra is the state itself. The state structures are the Russian mafia, arch-enemies of the written law and the people. The gang of former party and Komsomol functionaries have divided up Russia's natural resources between themselves, and are desperate to sell them as quickly as possible so that they can acquire instant wealth, without giving any thought to others or to their own country's future. Rather than being invested in Russian roads, hospitals and schools, the money they earn from selling those resources flows westwards. The budget reserved by the state for social initiatives rarely reaches these, and instead percolates into the pockets of officials. A principle no more complex than 'Climb the ladder, and help yourself' has become the new Russia's ideology. Corruption is not an exception to the rule, but the rule itself. No wonder, then, that the blogger and opposition leader Alexei Navalny has pithily called the ruling party, United Russia, a 'party of crooks and thieves'.

The fact that Russian society is corrupt is nothing new – it always has been. In the absence of independent courts and without clear legislation, problems have never been resolved with the help of abstract bureaucratic regulations, but by means of direct communication and mutual understanding: 'You scratch my back, I'll scratch yours.' It may seem odd, but the system of bribery grants Russians an immense freedom, allowing them to solve their problems in the quickest and most efficient way possible. The system of corruption has survived any attempt at modernisation. This smoothly functioning social order switches between 'socialisms' and 'capitalisms' as often as it changes its clothes. You can buy a new T-shirt or wash an old one, but your body's metabolism will remain the same. In the new Russia, the system has merely been nationalised. The age of Yeltsin took crooks and bandits from their Soviet suburbs and introduced them as Russia's new elite. People with a criminal bent were now in charge of the country's fortunes.

To survive in prison, you need to have certain qualities, a certain mental constitution. In Russia, the qualities you need to survive are being passed down from one generation to the next. Russians have experienced prison life both metaphorically and literally: a quarter of the population has been in prison, or has had a family member in prison. Prison customs have a huge influence on the young – not to forget the guards, and their families. Recent statistics show that nearly 400,000 people make their living in the penal system; prison slang, the criminal subculture and the normative power of 'prison morality' not only influence modern Russian society, but provide its very foundations. Prison knows only one law – the law of strength and violence. It is the unwritten law by which people in Russia have always lived.

Russian sociologists describe the influence prison culture has on society as 'prisonisation', a neologism derived from the English word 'prison' but which also sounds utterly Russian: *pri zone* means something like 'at the zone' or 'by the zone' – and the whole country lives under the zone's influence. There has always been a prison camp mentality in Russia: criminals from the upper echelons of society get the best bunks in the cell, take clothes and food from the weak, and maintain order – a criminal order. The only kind there is.

They say that prisons, armies and schools reflect the essence of the society around them. Society in the Golden Horde's Moscow ulus was modelled on a prison from the start, and it was in the days of the Mongols that the tripartite hierarchy of interaction between those in power and their subjects was born: on the first step stands the prison governor (the Mongol khan), who rules over life and death. Inside the 'zone' are two further steps, the first of which is occupied by privileged inmates (the princes who received the *yarlyk* from the khan), who act as guards, and right at the bottom are the common convicts (the rank and file). In this kind of society, there are no laws or contracts, no rights or regulations, only favour and disfavour, privileges and oppression. And when the people revolt, they don't call for 'your and our freedom' – as in the Polish wars of liberation from the Russian tsar – but for a new, 'real' tsar – as in Pugachev's peasants' revolt, which drew the following comment from Pushkin: 'God spare us from Russian revolt, senseless merciless Russian revolt.'*

Prison teaches you how to be a slave, and when you leave prison a 'free' man, you take its rules with you. You store the trauma you have suffered – the brutality, torture and degradation, the division into guards and slaves – and pass these

---

* Alexander Pushkin, *The Captain's Daughter*, trans. Robert Chandler and Elizabeth Chandler (New York: New York Review Books, 2014), p. 130.

experiences on to family, friends and others. Everyday conflicts in Russia are shockingly brutal. Tolerance is practically unknown.

It didn't take long for 'prisonisation' to invade the official language. With the new rulers in the Kremlin, prison jargon entered public discourse – such as Putin's famous manifesto promise, made when he was still crown prince and trying to woo the Russian people, that he would 'drown the Chechens in the crapper'. Ever since, prison slang has been an invariable component of the Russian political elite's public statements, and words such as *zanoz* and *otkat* (variations on the payment of bribes) have entered the official vocabulary alongside hundreds of other expressions from the criminal underworld.

The code of behaviour inside the zone also shapes behaviour outside it. Take smiling, for example: Western tourists' first impression of Russians is of an unfriendly and stand-offish people. In Russia, people rarely smile at strangers. In the West, they usually make brief eye contact and wear the suggestion of a smile, but in Russia the non-committal smile is more or less unknown. I, too, would instinctively put on a grumpy expression the moment I left the house. People feel that they are in an aggressive environment, so the moment they get outside they put on a protective mask and prepare to defend themselves. It is the prison mentality: behind bars, it's fine to smile at fellow inmates you know well, but smile at anyone else and you're seen as a weakling fawning over those who are stronger than you. If someone approaches you with a smile, you recoil – they seem sneaky, dirty. I learnt all this from my brother, when I visited him up north in Ivdel.

What unites the people either side of the barbed wire more than anything is the feeling of helplessness when faced with people in authority.

Anything that prison hasn't taught you, you learn in the army. The army is another important access point for a Russian's 'sentimental education'. Interestingly, in Russia the army is seen as playing a civilising role: at the end of the nineteenth century, a Russian general declared that 'forty per cent of the lads have eaten meat for the first time in their lives in the army'; and at the start of the twenty-first, on 15 February 2006, defence minister Sergei Ivanov told the Duma: 'For some recruits, it's the first time they see a toilet bowl, a toothbrush and three meals a day. It's not easy, training soldiers like that.'

In Russia, the army is not only a cultural institution, but a school for slaves. Key to this are the so-called unprescribed behavioural rules – its unbreakable and unwritten laws. A soldier's rank depends on the time he has served. Older soldiers practically have unlimited power over new recruits; they exploit their position daily by forcing recruits to perform tough tasks, and abuse and humiliate novices in rituals that are unanimously approved. If you want to survive, you first have to become a slave and let go of your human dignity. After a while, you are promoted from slave to master, and then it's your turn to beat up the newbies, piss into their boots, make them eat a slice of bread smeared with shoe polish, take away the food parcels their families have sent them, and much more. It is a truism that former slaves make the most brutal guards. Later, these 'unprescribed behavioural rules' are applied to life at large. Most Russian men are graduates of this school for slaves, and they carry their newly acquired skills and expertise with them into family life.

But there was and is a different Russia too: the Russia of Alexander Pushkin and Anton Chekhov, of Pyotr Chaadayev and Alexander Herzen, of Leo Tolstoy and Marc Chagall, of Sergei Rachmaninov and Daniil Kharms, of Andrei Tarkovsky and Lev Kopelev, of Alfred Schnittke and Joseph Brodsky; the Russia of those seven young women and men, who went to Red Square in August 1968 to protest against Soviet tanks in Prague, where they unfurled a banner with the words 'For your and our freedom' only to be arrested on the spot. I was seven then, and knew nothing about it. Indeed, no one anywhere in our huge country heard about what they did. Their lives were destroyed, and they spent years in prison or in psychiatric hospital. One Czech journalist commented, 'Seven people in Red Square is at least seven reasons why we will never be able to hate the Russians again.'

When, in the 1930s, Boris Pasternak was asked to put his name to a letter demanding the execution of 'enemies of the people', his pregnant wife fell down at his feet and begged him to sign it for the sake of their child. He replied, 'If I sign this, I will be a different person. And I don't care about the fate of someone else's child.' It wasn't heroism, it was something else:

an inability to be untrue to yourself. An inability to be someone other than who you are.

A month before his death, Boris Nemtsov, who was murdered near the Kremlin in 2015, said in an interview: 'Everyone has to decide for themselves whether they're prepared to take risks or not. I can only speak for myself. I'm glad that I can speak the truth, that I can be true to myself and don't have to grovel before the wretched, thieving state authorities. Freedom is expensive.'

This other Russia began with Pushkin, which is why the poet is so important to Russians. The century that passed between Russia's opening up to Western influence under Peter the Great and the arrival of Pushkin was an age of preparation, of profound internal maturation. The Moscow ulus was filling up with European foreigners, who brought with them not only technology and other equipment, fashions and languages, but also their culture, literature and ideas. It was only a question of time before the Russian language internalised Western thoughts, and before the emergence of Russians with European notions of human dignity – 'Russian Europeans', as Dostoevsky called them in *The Adolescent*.

The newly awakened consciousness of the first Russian Europeans was not very happy about its awakening. As Pushkin once said, 'What a devil's trick that I should have been born with a soul and talent in Russia!' His role was to show how someone with a soul and talent could live in a place where it was impossible to survive if you had a soul and talent. He was a Russian Moses, bringing his people the commandments they needed to live with dignity. He had not been summoned to a mountaintop, no hand emerged from a cloud to hand him tablets of stone – he simply lived, and the commandments were the stanzas of his poetry and his life.

Born into a country where serfdom was nothing more than the formal expression of a profound mental enslavement experienced by serfs and masters alike, he enacted a fundamental Russian transformation, a peculiar Russian revolution: to the pyramid of power, at whose apex stood the tsar who controlled the fate of nations great and small, he juxtaposed a pyramid at whose apex stood the poet. With that, he inaugurated a key theme in Russian culture, 'the poet versus the tsar'. To the traditional Russian system of omnipotence – where everyone was, as Peter the Great put it, a 'soldier in the fatherland's army' or, as Beria called them, 'camp dust' – Pushkin juxtaposed another kind of power, hitherto unknown in Russia: the power of the free creative mind. From this point on, the hierarchy of imperial consciousness epitomised by Peter the Great's 'Table of Ranks' had to contend with a hierarchy that was subject to no law, but which nevertheless everyone, including the tsar, acknowledged:

I have erected a monument not built by hand.
    The people's path to it will never become overgrown;
It has raised its defiant head higher
    Than the Alexander Column.

Russia's political rulers were now afraid of poets, who, following Pushkin, themselves constituted a powerful force. The other Russia was born.

Pushkin's verse novel *Eugene Onegin* will always be relevant in Russia, because it is about human dignity, the greatest of all human values. It is more valuable than love. That is why Tatyana rejects Onegin. It is more valuable than life, and that is why Lensky has to die. Perhaps this is the most important lesson that Pushkin taught this country, where you are debased every step of the way, from the day you are born until the day you die: you must guard human dignity with your life. No one can be taught how to do this; you can only lead by example. Which is what he did, with that duel on the banks of St Petersburg's Black River. Pushkin's death was his final commandment. The Russian versifiers who went before him did not know that a poet's death is his last word. Pushkin resisted all his friend's efforts to prevent the duel, because he knew his death would form an integral – indeed, the most essential – part of his work. Both Lensky and his creator could have avoided their duels, but for both it was the only way to defend their human dignity.

Many years later, in August 1968, it was precisely for this reason that those young people, who barely got the chance to unfurl their banners, risked their lives in Red Square: they saw no other way to defend their human dignity. A thread led from Red Square back to the Black River.

The Russian Europeans of the nineteenth century, both

Westerners and Slavophiles, felt the Golden Horde's degrading psychological legacy. The poet Nikolai Shcherbina (1821–1869) wrote: 'We represent European words and Asian behaviour.' The historian and public intellectual Mikhail Pogodin (1800–1875) wrote: 'We are Tatars from head to toe. When there is no one to give us direct orders, we are unhappy. We don't know what to do with our hands and feet, and end up ordering ourselves around, as roughly and aggressively as possible.' Nikolai Kostomarov (1817–1885), one of Russia's best-known historians, wrote this about the consequences of Mongol rule: 'Any sense of freedom, honour and personal dignity dissipated, and deference to authority and despotism towards your subordinates became part of the Russian soul.' This devastating realisation inevitably triggered a revolt from Russian Europeans, and its result was the Russian intelligentsia.

The intelligentsia was neither a social class nor a political party; rather, it was a quasi-religious community of like-minded people, who saw it as their mission to liberate Russia from autocracy. Its members radically rejected the existing conditions, and advocated a revolution that would sweep away the unjust 'Asian' order and secure freedoms and rights for Russian citizens. A feeling of guilt towards the uneducated and passive population played an important part in this, and the ultimate aim was to enlighten people and educate them in European values. Freedom was the intelligentsia's religion, and they saw themselves as its missionaries in Russia, as a kind of guiding moral authority. They displayed qualities that were alien to the traditional Russian system: initiative, civil responsibility, social critique, a social conscience, sympathy for the 'humiliated and insulted' (as one of Dostoevsky's early novels is called) and empathy towards the 'uncivilised' peasant population. On the one hand, they declared war on the Moscow ulus and championed democratic values, yet on the other, they and their arch-enemy were spiritually related: the intelligentsia produced the professional revolutionaries who countered the injustice of tyranny with the 'justice' of revolutionary violence. They thought terror morally acceptable, and their terrorists climbed the scaffold under the halo of martyrdom.

The intelligentsia were intolerant, uncompromising and utterly convinced that they were right. They had a predilection for total confrontation, and were always ready to brand, to unmask, to incite. It took an unusual degree of civil courage to openly advocate a policy of compromise. The object of their relentless hate were those in power, yet at the same time they fervently yearned to be in power themselves. Any concession on the part of the government radicalised the intelligentsia further, and they hunted the reformist 'liberator tsar' Alexander II like a wild animal. The war against tsarism was dictated by its own logic: the more liberal the system of power became and the more of the opposition's demands were met, the more ruthlessly they attacked the retreating enemy.

The intelligentsia's willingness to sacrifice themselves led to a willingness to sacrifice others for their lofty ideals too. Dozens of innocent people lost their lives in numerous attacks on the tsar and high-ranking officials, but the intelligentsia considered them – in modern parlance – 'collateral damage'. The idea of assassinating the tsar obsessed them for several generations. When Zinaida Gippius, a poet and leading intellectual of the Russian 'Silver Age' (the name philologists gave to the first two decades of the twentieth century, which, after the nineteenth century's 'Golden Age', were particularly fruitful for poetry), heard that Nicholas II had been shot dead, she wrote in her diary that 'I certainly feel no pity for that feeble little officer'. The intelligentsia considered the assassination of the tsar as something like an act of deliverance.

The suffering populace were the intelligentsia's sacred cow. The fight for its well-being justified every sacrifice. At the same time, they were positively convinced that they knew what was good for the people better than the suffering people did themselves. They believed they had the right to steer this uneducated mass and lead it towards happiness. The 'populist' Narodniks' attempts to disseminate propaganda among the rural population failed miserably, because the people merely saw them as troublemakers and enemies of the tsar who wanted to insert themselves into the embrace in which people and ruler were locked.

The intelligentsia were not synonymous with the educated classes – only those who were against the regime could call themselves members. But many Russian Europeans thought that, in a Russian context, Western ideas were inappropriate and damaging. In their view, it was not the case that the Russian empire ran counter to what people wanted; rather, it aligned with people's desire for, and expectations of, patriarchy. They argued that the revolutionary war against the state would be a catastrophe, because in Russia a strong government was the guarantor of civilisation. They believed with Pushkin that the government was 'the only European in Russia', and that without an iron fist and a strict power structure, Russia would not witness a free and peaceful society, but only the kind of senseless and merciless uprising that Pushkin warned about (and which took place in 1917). They saw the government as a bulwark between the archaic masses, with their archaic mentality, and the thin layer of educated, Europeanised people. The last thing they wanted was revolution. But the intelligentsia labelled the writers and philosophers who held such views, and who included Dostoevsky and Konstantin Leontiev, as reactionaries.

When the tsarist regime went into liquidation, the intelligentsia didn't have long to celebrate their epoch-making victory. They had idealised the suffering masses and fought to liberate this imagined people, but now they were confronted with the reality. The poet Alexander Blok sang the praises of revolution, but the peasants burnt down his priceless library; and in the summer of 1917, the composer Rachmaninov was horrified by the living conditions on his Ivanovka estate, which were 'such that, after spending three weeks there, I have resolved never to return'. The final straw came when the peasants he once loved so much gruesomely killed his daughter's favourite dog with a spade. Rachmaninov's grand piano was thrown out of a second-floor window, and Ivanovka was reduced to ashes. The same thing happened to almost every Russian estate, those artificial islands where generations of Russian Europeans had grown up. The archipelago of European culture was engulfed by bloody waves of revolutionary anarchy. The intelligentsia had fulfilled its mission, the despotic tsarist regime had collapsed, Russia was proclaimed a democratic republic and the people won all kinds of freedoms – but dread and fear were the aftermath. The Bolsheviks were already busy creating another archipelago: the Gulag Archipelago.

Following the October Revolution of 1917, parts of the Russian European contingent were brutally crushed, others went into exile; the rest had to find ways to adapt to the new regime, and trembled. Experts in science and technology were indispensable, and former tsarist officers, technicians and engineers were incorporated into the armed forces, administration and industry as so-called civilian specialists – but only until the old guard could be replaced by new 'Soviet' specialists drawn from the proletariat and the peasant population.

A countless number of the old intelligentsia fell victim to the Great Purge. The dictatorship wanted to eradicate all those who had European notions of freedom. The few Russian Europeans who survived were forced to pursue a clandestine existence in Stalin's Soviet Union, always afraid of being unmasked and hounded. Persecution campaigns were a constant – whether against 'an anti-patriotic group of theatre critics', 'rootless

cosmopolitans', 'lickspittles of the West' or 'formalist composers'. On 15 February 1948, the world-famous composer
Sergei Prokofiev wrote a letter to the Chair of the Committee
for the Arts, which ran as follows:

> I welcome the resolution of the Central Committee of the
> CPSU, which creates the conditions necessary to restore the
> health of the entire organism of Soviet music. The resolu-
> tion is particularly important because it points out that the
> formalist movement, which leads to the impoverishment
> and decadence of music, is alien to the Soviet people, and
> because it clearly indicates the aims we must pursue to best
> serve the Soviet people . . . The existence of formalism in
> some of my works can probably be explained by an insuf-
> ficient vigilance and a failure to realise that our people in
> no way need it. Yet after the announcement of the Central
> Committee's resolution, which has shaken every single one
> among us composers to the core, it is now clear what kind of
> music our people needs, and with what methods we can fight
> the disease of formalism . . . Furthermore, I wish to express
> my gratitude to the Party for the clear guidelines provided
> by its resolution, which will help me on my search for an
> accessible musical language appropriate to our people, and
> worthy of our people and our great country.

Four days after Prokofiev posted the letter, on 20 February
1948, his wife Lina Codina was arrested.

After the revolution, the meaning of the term 'intelligentsia' changed. Now, all academics were part of the 'Soviet intelligentsia', which constituted a new social class of highly educated people, alongside the working class and the kolkhoz peasant class.

The post-Stalin generations were extremely interested in Western culture; its music, fashions and literature percolated into the Soviet Union through the tiniest holes and tears in the Iron Curtain. The Soviet intelligentsia, however, shared only a few features with its pre-revolutionary incarnation. More than anything, they were so intimidated that they lacked the will to protest against the regime, which prompted Solzhenitsyn to write his famous article 'Obrazovanshina' ('The Smatterers'). Before the revolution, intellectual anti-state activists were a mass phenomenon. Now, only a few dozen representatives of the Soviet intelligentsia were willing to protest openly. They called them 'dissidents'.

The credo adopted by these freedom fighters came from the prison camps: 'Don't trust, don't fear, don't beg!' was the inmates' law in the Gulag, which Solzhenitsyn turned into the code of conduct for every honourable person living in this prison country.

The dissidents were the few free people among the slaves. The difference between free people and slaves is that free people take responsibility for their country. Ordinary Soviet citizens felt not in the least accountable for the crimes committed by their country, such as the bloody suppression of the

Hungarian uprising in 1956, the occupation of Czechoslovakia in 1968 and the invasion of Afghanistan in 1979. The ulus's subjects did not feel responsible for the actions of the state. The dissidents, though, did. Was it the fault of the seven young people in Red Square in August 1968 that Russian tanks rolled through Prague? Was Andrei Dmitrievich Sakharov, member of the Science Academy, to blame for Russian aggression in Afghanistan? Nonetheless, they felt shame at their homeland's base actions. Being ashamed of your own country is the first step on the long road to freedom. These people saved their honour, and that of their fellow citizens, with this self-sacrificial protest. After Soviet troops marched into Czechoslovakia, the poet and singer Alexander Galich sang, 'Countrymen! The fatherland is in danger! Our tanks are rolling into a foreign country!' Most Soviet citizens simply didn't get it – and those who did were too scared to protest openly. They all had mouths to feed. Having mouths to feed explains and justifies a lot.

A hundred years ago, the 'populists' were seen by their own people as aliens and enemies of the state. Likewise, the dissidents were accused by millions of their fellow Soviet citizens of dirtying the nest, of being traitors and foreign agents. But these brave people were vilified even more, and more mercilessly, by their own colleagues. The Soviet Writers' Union unanimously (!) expelled Pasternak in 1958 for writing *Doctor Zhivago* and receiving the Nobel Prize, and persecuted the great author like a pack of wolves. Interestingly, that same year, three Russian scientists – Igor Tamm, Pavel Cherenkov and Ilya

Frank – were awarded the Nobel Prize in Physics; the country's leading physicists published an open letter in *Pravda*, saying that they were proud of the Physics prize, but outraged that the Swedish Academy honoured Pasternak in what they described as a 'dirty act of political provocation'. Representatives from all corners of Soviet intelligentsia actively participated in the persecution campaign that doubtless accelerated Pasternak's illness and eventual death.

The author Daniil Granin is well known in Germany for his January 2014 Bundestag speech about the siege of Leningrad. In Russia, he is remembered as a particularly crass example of a Soviet intellectual who, in order to survive and to be able to work on his wonderful books, assisted in several of the sorts of malicious acts that the state invited people to perpetrate at the time. In 1964, he participated in a persecution campaign against Brodsky which led to the poet's arrest and enforced exile, and in 1969 he voted for Solzhenitsyn to be thrown out of the Writers' Union for *The Gulag Archipelago*. A few years before his death in 2017, he told an interviewer: 'My conscience is my business. I saw that I couldn't help Solzhenitsyn, and would only destroy myself – so I joined in. And I don't regret it.' This plain statement says a lot about the Russian mentality.

It perhaps also explains why the Soviet people and Soviet intelligentsia hated the dissidents: a slave can never forgive a free person their freedom. 'Freedom is expensive. Not everyone can afford it.'

The hugely popular Russian-Georgian philosopher Merab

Mamardashvili (1930–1990) wrote in 1979 that 'you could declare Russia a parliamentary democracy today, but nothing would work. Freedom cannot be a gift. It takes people who need, understand and act on that freedom, who simply can't live without freedom.' When the Soviet Union fell and people were given their freedom, there clearly weren't enough of them who needed, understood and acted on that freedom, who simply couldn't live without freedom.

Alexander Griboyedov, one of the first Russian Europeans, wrote a famous comedy called *Wit Begets Woe* (1823), which remains the most performed play in Russia – a fact that shows how relevant it still is. Chatsky, the hero of this verse drama, has just returned from western Europe and feels lost in Russian society, misunderstood and maligned. He is an alien guest at the Russian feast, and all he does is keep others from happily vegetating away their lives. In Russia, reason, knowledge, culture, intelligence and discernment make people unhappy.

When I was a kid, I read a short story in an anthology called *Phantastic-72* which for some reason made a big impression on me, even though I didn't quite understand what the author was getting at. The story went like this: an Earthling is out for a walk. He meets a strange creature, which introduces itself as a Martian. To prove its origins, the Martian does something alien-like. The Earthling is flabbergasted. He asks why Earthlings haven't been able to spot any traces of its civilisation on the surface of Mars. The Martian replies, 'We have set up invisible facilities everywhere, so that we can watch the development of human civilisation unseen.' Human civilisation, it tells him, is evolving in entirely the wrong direction. Humans wage wars, treat each other with brutality, and feel too little sympathy, mercy or love – it'll end badly. The short story concludes with the Martian saying, 'And now, you must forget everything I've told you, and that we ever met.' The Earthling thinks to himself, 'What a nice day! Maybe I'll go fishing.'

I think I know now what the author was trying to say.

Chapter 9

'Here's to the Patience of the Great Russian People!'

Several years ago, a book tour took me to Tromsø, a small city in Norway's far north. I had some time to kill before a public reading, so I went for a walk, where I passed a small local museum. It was sheer coincidence – or proof that there is no such thing. In two of its rooms, there was an exhibition about Russian prisoners of war in Norway during the Second World War. As the Germans retreated from Finland, they moved their prison camps to the area around Tromsø, and in the display cabinets were old documents, clothes, spoons and other utensils, and photos. I was the only one there. I was studying a yellowed map when, suddenly, the word 'Kandalaksha' flashed through my mind. It was a word from my childhood.

When I was little, I would spend every summer at my

grandmother's. She lived in our family's dacha in Udelnaya, just outside Moscow. Old photos hung on the wall in her room. One of them was of her sons – my father and his older brother Boris, Uncle Borya; two adolescents with sticky-out ears sitting next to each other, arm in arm, head to head, ears touching. Nowadays, people grin stiffly in photos, but the boys' faces are serious as they look into the lens, as if they knew what was coming. In another photo, Borya was wearing headphones – he loved working with radios, and had qualified as a telephonist.

I can see my grandmother now, unfolding and kissing the tattered death notice and wiping tears from her eyes. Uncle Borya was twenty years old. When I think of my own sons, I realise how young he was, a kid really. Back then, though, the Uncle Borya in that photo seemed to me like a big, grown-up hero.

Strictly speaking, the frayed, yellowed piece of paper didn't announce Borya's death, only that he had been declared missing near Kandalaksha. Missing. The strange name of Kandalaksha, a town in Karelia, stuck in my mind. I think that, for as long as she lived, my grandmother harboured the hope that her Borya might not be dead, that he might still be alive somewhere. Missing – what did it actually mean? It could mean anything. Perhaps he was alive, and she would see him again some day. My father, too, hoped that his brother was still alive. My grandmother died in 1993, my father in 1995.

And now something happened that only ever happens in

films or books, never in real life. I was standing there, alone in a museum in the far north of Norway, and a place with the strange name 'Kandalaksha', marked on an old map, had me spellbound. I wondered: if Uncle Borya was taken prisoner there, might he have been among the POWs relocated to Norway in 1944? That same evening, back in my hotel room after the reading, I emailed a few questions to the Norwegian National Archives. A few days later they sent me a scan of Boris Shishkin's POW registration card: *Identity card*, issued on 29 August 1941. *Stalag 309*. 'Stalag' as in the *Stammlager*, German POW camps; '309' stood for the network of camps in Finland. Each POW was given a tag made of tin, and his was number 1249. *Shishkin, Boris, born 30 December 1920 in Novoyuryevo. Father's given name: Mikhail.* Mikhail Shishkin, my grandfather, who was arrested in 1930. *Nationality: Russian. Rank . . . Unit . . . Normal occupation: Radio mechanic. Captured on 27 August. Whether healthy, ill or wounded: h'y. Fingerprint, r/h index. Name and address of next of kin in the prisoner's homeland: Mother, Lyubov Shishkina* – my grandmother. Her address: *Town: Ilyinka. Region: Moscow.* As I read the card, I realised what it feels like to have someone resurrected from the dead. This man, my twenty-year-old uncle, a mere child compared to me, his grey-haired nephew – suddenly, he was alive again. The fact that my grandmother and my father never lived to see this day made it all the more painful.

Naturally, I immediately started searching online – since there's nothing you can't find there – for information about

Stalag 309. I found images, articles, documents, stories from people who had been held there and survived. I even saw photos of men being shot dead, secretly taken by a German soldier. I read that most POWs were put to work building a railway, and somewhere they also mentioned telephonists. Surely he was one of them! It only stood to reason that they would employ POWs where they'd be most useful, based on their skills.

On the back of the card, I spotted these strange words: *Statements made by an informant suggest that the prisoner of war may be Jewish. Handed over to the security police on 25.7.1942.*

This could only mean that they'd executed him.

On a website dedicated to Stalag 309, there's a photo of dead POWs lying in a large pit. Perhaps my father's brother is among them.

I can't describe what it felt like to see my uncle Borya resurrected – only for him to be instantly executed again.

My next thought was that perhaps it was better, after all, that my father and grandmother were no longer around and didn't have to go through this.

It was strange, too, that they'd murdered him because they thought he was a Jew – him, a Russian peasant from an old Tambov family. Probably someone out to settle an old score. One person's denunciation was all it took to get yourself executed.

That photo from my childhood no longer exists. Our family archive was destroyed fifteen years ago, when my brother's dacha burnt down. I can still picture it clearly, that pre-war photo of the boy in headphones – but it doesn't exist anywhere in the world any more, it seems, only in my head.

Another remarkable thing is that someone had added a hand-written Russian translation of the details on the card. Who had done this, and when, and for what purpose? There's a Russian stamp emblazoned on the card too: *Updated details added to personnel file, reference no. 452*. And then the word 'notified', again written by hand, most likely meaning the piece of paper my grandmother wept over for all those years.

I soon found the answer: after the war, all German archives containing documents relating to Russian POWs were passed to the Soviet Union, and since they contained all sorts of information of interest to the Russian secret service they were translated right away. The files are still in the military archives in Podolsk, near Moscow. My grandmother and my father spent all those years not knowing what became of Boris, and it was their own fatherland that had kept his fate secret from them, the same fatherland for which my father and his brother fought in the war. They only opened the archives during perestroika, to allow Western historians to copy the files. The Norwegian archive had sent me the scan in less than a week, but their own state had deprived my father and my grandmother of this information their whole lives.

Why did the state keep the information it had about POWs secret for decades? Because it was in reality conducting a war against its own people. My relatives, the people closest to me, were exploited by the state for its wars, and the state had nothing but contempt for them.

While my father fought against the evil of fascism, he was exploited by another evil. He and the millions of other Soviet soldiers were slaves, and rather than liberating the world they had helped introduce a new kind of slavery. The people sacrificed everything for victory, but the fruits of that victory were poverty and even greater oppression. Victory gave the slaves nothing but a sense of the greatness of their master's empire. The great victory of 1945 only cemented their profound enslavement.

My father was four when the GPU (the Soviet Union's secret police from 1922 to 1934) arrested his father. Sons want to be proud of their fathers, but how can you be proud of an enemy of the people? Whenever he had to fill in a form, my father never mentioned that he was the son of an enemy of the people, and was always scared that some day it would come out. All he would put is 'father deceased'. Fear, not pride, settled in my father's soul, and poisoned it.

No matter its prevailing ideology at any given time, the Russian regime always used patriotism to manipulate its people. What makes it so perfidious is that it was, and still is, exploiting one of the most wonderful human emotions – loving your country, being ready to sacrifice everything for it. Those in power take the place of the homeland: my father went to war to defend his homeland, but he was really defending the regime that had murdered his father.

When perestroika was in full swing, my father submitted a request to the KGB for information about his father's fate. During that time, those who died in Stalin's purges were rehabilitated, and he once showed me the official letter that confirmed that his father, my grandfather Mikhail Shishkin, was also rehabilitated. The letter said that proceedings against him had been abandoned due to 'a lack of evidence'.

The morning the letter arrived, my father started drinking early. He just kept slurring, 'Pigs! . . . Murderers!'

The regime's tactic of using patriotism to manipulate people has worked perfectly every time – in the tsarist empire, in the Soviet empire, and in the modernised Moscow ulus of the twenty-first century. There was only one brief interval, after 1917, when the word 'patriotism' acquired a wholly negative meaning for the Bolsheviks. Marxist dogma taught that the proletariat didn't have a fatherland, that only the International promised deliverance. But loving the 'socialist fatherland' became part of Soviet propaganda as early as the mid-1930s, when Stalin revised Marx and prioritised 'socialism in one country'. When the Second World War broke out, the international solidarity of the proletariat was forgotten. When Soviet–German hostilities broke out in June 1941, the browbeaten people suddenly heard the loudspeakers proclaim, 'Brothers and Sisters!' – and Soviet propaganda, hitherto directed against everything Russian and Orthodox, turned patriotic, calling on the people to kill not the fascists, but the Germans. Instead of the proletariat, it was the great Russian people who would now be the progressive force in human history.

At the gala reception held in the Kremlin on 24 May 1945 in honour of the Red Army's military leaders, Stalin made his now famous toast, 'To the patience of the great Russian people!' The dictator admitted that 'our government has made its share of mistakes. In 1941–1942, there were many moments when the situation was desperate, when our army retreated and gave up our beloved and cherished villages and towns in Ukraine, Belarus, Moldavia, around Leningrad, in the Baltic countries and the Karelo-Finnish Republic, because there was no other way out. A different people might have said to their government: "You have not lived up to our expectations. Clear off – we will install a new government that will make peace with Germany and secure peace for our country." But the Russian people did not do that . . .' As it turned out, the most important outcome of the Great Patriotic War was that power remained in the hands of the Khan of Khans.

Patriotism governed proceedings after the war too. Patriots decoded the Russian pseudonyms of Jewish artists and incited the persecution of Jews; following Stalin's death, Russian patriots hounded 'anti-patriots' such as the Nobel laureates Boris Pasternak, Aleksandr Solzhenitsyn and Joseph Brodsky, the physicist and dissident Andrei Sakharov, the ballet dancers Rudolf Nureyev and Mikhail Baryshnikov, the virtuoso cellist Mstislav Rostropovich and the opera singer Galina Vishnevskaya, the Taganka Theatre's director Yuri Lyubimov and the film director Andrei Tarkovsky. It would take a long time to list the names of all the 'Russian traitors' among the cultural elite.

These days, Russian propaganda flatters TV audiences into believing that the biggest names in world culture belong to Russia: Tolstoy, Dostoevsky, Tchaikovsky, Shostakovich, and many other artists, writers, composers and directors. They all belong to us! That's who we are, we Russians, we're the most gifted of all, a nation of geniuses! No one mentions, or indeed gives any thought at all to, the fact that most Russian cultural figures have left behind a trail of such brilliance not thanks to the state, but despite it, despite the regimes' contempt for humanity. They gladly identify with Russia's great culture – which the current regime has thus appropriated.

The Russian people's patriotism is the identical twin of its sense of debasement. When you feel debased, you seek some sort of compensation. Slaves are proud of their masters' wealth and status. This compensation mechanism worked perfectly in the Soviet era, when they would proudly announce on the radio that 'it is for this that we have built rockets and dammed the Yenisey'. Generations grew up with the slogan 'Long live the great Soviet people – the builders of communism!', and pupils would be shown with the help of a map that Russia was the biggest country in the world. When I was in primary school, I, too, was proud of the size of my homeland. We knew that we were the biggest, best and mightiest people in the world, and that the enemy trembled before our army. But children can be forgiven for believing things like that.

The Russian inferiority complex is invisible, but manifest. Take, for just one example, the fact that no company would ever use the word 'Russian' in an advert to highlight the quality of its goods or services. That would be more like an anti-advert. This shows just what the people think of themselves, their quality of life and their ability to create a competitive product. And they compensate for their low self-esteem with a grand patriotic hauteur.

Every day, they are degraded by officials who belittle them as nonentities, by volatile nouveau riche criminals, by the country's abysmal medical care, demeaning pensions and a general feeling of helplessness, and they need some kind of compensation. They find it in patriotic delusions of grandeur. What do the poor in Russia's rotting provinces have to be proud of? Well, there is still the fatherland and its victory.

The 9th of May used to play a special role in Soviet life. Living day in, day out in slavery, people were in dire need of periods when they could relax mentally, and say: We are the victors, and this is our victory! In the new Russia, the victory over Germany still (after more than seventy-five years! Other countries have long consigned the end of the Second World War to history) retains its compensatory significance, and is commemorated all the more enthusiastically for it. Once a year, the masses that have been deprived of their civilian rights are allowed to take to the streets and let it all out. 'We're a nation of winners!' 'We finished them all off!' 'We can do it again!' 'We are the mightiest, and we're right!' Pride in their Russianness oozes from their every pore.

They celebrate this one day as victors. The next, they are

already a defeated people again: the traffic cop extorts a bribe from you and the doctors in the hospital shrug and say, 'We don't have any medication here, you'll have to get hold of it somewhere else yourself,' while a mountain of rubbish piles up outside your house (but no one cares what you think).

In Putin's Russia, the 9th of May has nothing to do with the people's victory, my father's victory. When I was little, my father and I would spend the day out and about together, and in those days the slogan on the street was still 'Never again!' – not, like nowadays, 'We can do it again!' It is not a day of peace or a day of remembrance. It is a day of rattling weapons, a day of aggression, a day of war against foreigners and natives, a day of secret transports of dead bodies.

Every single regime used people's love for their fatherland as bait, and they will keep on doing it. Once more, a dictatorship, in order to protect itself, is calling on its subjects to defend the country, and mercilessly exploiting Russia's victory in the Great Patriotic War. They stole oil from my own people, stole their elections, stole their civil rights, stole their country. And they stole their victory.

When oil prices were high, those in power were able to feed the people with crumbs from their table. Political scientists called the 2000s the 'fat years' of the social contract that the state had silently made with the people, which stipulated that the latter gave up their civil rights for prosperity and stability. When the state's income from raw materials was drastically reduced, it reached for the magic wand of patriotism to bail itself out.

When the money runs out, there's nothing left for it but to exchange a generous social welfare policy for a rich spiritual life. Instead of distributing bread, they fed people patriotism.

When he was in power, Yeltsin called for a new national vision, but to no avail. His successor resolutely declared that 'we don't and can't have a unifying vision other than patriotism'. The satirist Mikhail Zhvanetsky described the new official Russian ideology thus: 'Patriotism is an explicit, clear and well-reasoned explanation for why our lives are worse than other people's.'

Hysterical calls emanate from every TV screen: 'Great, mighty Russia!' 'We are rising from our knees!' 'The return of Russian territories!' 'Defend our Russian language!' 'Gather Russian soil!' 'We won't give an inch!' And the Great Khan, of course, is right there at the front, leading the phalanx: on a horse, in a tank, on a submarine, on a plane. Again and again, the call goes out: 'Let's deliver the world from fascism.' Before our eyes, the Ukrainians were transformed into 'Ukrofascists', and Russians were once again called upon to defend their homeland from fascism. The war against the 'Ukronazis' and their Western accomplices was stylised as a new Great Patriotic War.

I remember seeing a report on TV when the Chechen war started, where a Russian soldier from Voronezh, practically still a boy, said, 'I am defending my homeland here.' Why was he defending his homeland against the Chechens in Chechnya? What were the Chechens defending there? This simple thought plainly hadn't entered his head. The propaganda machine can do whatever it wants with people, and now it wants young Russian and Ukrainian men to 'defend their homeland' against each other.

Today's propagandists of Russian patriotism seemingly learnt their trade from their Nazi colleagues. When Hermann Göring was interviewed by Gustave Gilbert in his prison cell in April 1946, Göring said: 'Of course, the ordinary people don't want war . . . But, after all, it is a country's leaders who determine policy, and it's always easy to get the people to join in, whether you're a democracy, a fascist dictatorship, a parliament or a communist dictatorship . . . It's really very simple. All you have to do is tell the people that they are under attack, accuse pacifists of a lack of patriotic feeling, and claim that they are putting the country at risk. It works in any country.'

As a side note, a popular talk show on Russian TV interpreted Dr Johnson's famous dictum that 'patriotism is the last refuge of a scoundrel' to mean that even the worst scoundrel has, somewhere in the darkness of their soul, a bright corner where their love for their homeland dwells. Johnson explained what he actually meant by it in his essay 'The Patriot' – but the Russian TV propagandists prefer their own version.

For the regime, war is the elixir of life. It brings with it a wave of patriotic feeling, and anyone who is unhappy about it can be vilified as a traitor of the people. So the regime has to create enemies – which is what TV propaganda is for, 'two minutes of hate' that last hours. But propaganda only works if people are willing to listen to it. It can only sprout in fertile soil.

There are plenty of alternative sources of information in Russia: websites run by opposition activists, for instance, or the prominent radio station Echo Moscow and the independent TV station Dozhd (a.k.a. TV Rain). Russians have to choose between two truths. The first goes like this: we Russians should be ashamed! We are being exploited by a criminal state, and once again licking the boots of bandits who have taken our country hostage. We are the aggressor, and our children are soldiers, killing and dying in eastern Ukraine, in a malicious war against a brother state which has chosen to embark on the road to democracy. The other declares: we are Russians, the only spiritual, indeed, sacred nation, which stands alone in its fight against American fascism. Our children are anti-fascists and heroes, sacrificing their lives to defend the Russian world, our homeland, and we are proud of them. Which truth would the parents of a soldier who has been killed in Ukraine and secretly buried choose?

The father of a paratrooper who returned from Ukraine without his legs posted this on Facebook: 'My son is a soldier. He did as he was ordered, so he did the right thing, no matter what happened to him, and I'm proud of him.' His human consciousness did not allow him to think that his son went off to murder his brothers; that he was not crippled while defending the fatherland from real enemies, but because of a mediocre lieutenant-colonel who is panicking, scared of losing his position of power, and because of the horde of ambitious thieves and embezzlers crowding his throne. After all, who finds it easy to admit that their own country, their own homeland, is a nasty aggressor and their own son . . . a fascist? The fatherland is surely always on the side of the angels. Once, the coffins that returned from Vietnam caused mass protests in the US. The coffins returning from the Ukraine will only lead to more coffins.

A Russian's 'patriotic' education starts with school. During the Soviet era, children were raised to believe in the cult of war and to glorify heroic military deeds. It's the same today. The Great Khan has personally intervened in the debate around the wording in history textbooks: 'We should never let anyone. make us feel guilty. It is the historians' task to instil a sense of pride in our country, especially among our young citizens.'

There are more than enough examples of this patriotic education in the new Russia. Let me cite just one: there is a very popular video clip on YouTube, of a Duma deputy and pupils from school No. 44 in Volgograd singing a song steeped in patriotism, which contains an item of sweeping geopolitical analysis: 'America is oppressing the people of the globe . . . the European Union has no mind of its own . . . the Middle East groans in its misery . . . the samurai will never get the Kuril Islands back . . . we will defend the amber capital [i.e. Kaliningrad] to the death . . . we will guide Alaska back into its home port.' The key message is repeated in the chorus: 'And when the commander-in-chief calls us to make a last stand, Uncle Vova, we'll stand with you!' It's hard to believe that it isn't meant as a joke or scathing satire. They are being deadly serious.

Leo Tolstoy's portrait hangs in every Russian school. In Russia, they honour him, but they don't read him. His great name is invoked as part of the patriotic curriculum, but teachers are unlikely to be brave enough to read out these lines from 'Patriotism and Christianity' to their pupils:

The government assures the people that they are in danger of being attacked by another country or by an enemy in their midst, and that the only way to escape lies is slavish obedience to the government. This fact is particularly evident in times of revolution and dictatorship, but it exists always and everywhere that the power of the government exists . . . Once the government has assured the people of the danger it is in, it subjects them to its control and, once they are in its control, compels them to attack other nations . . . According to its simplest, clearest and most unequivocal definition, patriotism is nothing but a means for rulers to satisfy their ambitions and desires; for the ruled, it means the abdication of all human dignity, reason and self-awareness, and their slavish subjugation to those in power. Patriotism thus obtains wherever it is preached. Patriotism is slavery.

Or these, from 'Patriotism and Government': 'People should understand that patriotic feeling, which alone shores up this instrument of violation [i.e. the government], is a crass, injurious, ignominious, iniquitous feeling, and above all immoral.'

But what does it actually mean to be a patriot? Again, the West has misunderstood: in Russia, patriotism means obedience and loyalty to higher-ranking patriots. Critics of the regime are accused of being Russophobes, of dirtying the nest and seeking to discredit Russia. What can discredit Russia more than the actions of the Russian government? Those who are in power are the ones discrediting my country, not the people who condemn their crimes. Patriotism is Russia's sacred cow, and it chews the cud of human rights and respect for the individual.

Following perestroika, Brodsky, my favourite poet – who was forced into exile by the Soviet government – was eulogised by the new 'democratic' Russia, and repeatedly invited to return, including by the then mayor of St Petersburg personally. Brodsky never did come back, and his grave is not in the city of his birth. Was he a bad patriot? He is the Russian language's pride and joy. Now, state patriots want to appropriate him, and his fame too, and keep quoting a poem by him in which he refers to the Ukrainian poet Taras Shevchenko somewhat condescendingly. If Brodsky were to be resurrected, I am certain that he would emigrate again just to make sure that these patriots don't honour him. The most important of all Russian questions is this: if the fatherland is a monster, should you love or hate it? It encompasses everything, inextricably. The regime has always done everything in its power to intertwine itself with the homeland in the minds of its people. As a famous line by the noted nineteenth-century poet Nikolai Nekrasov has it, 'A heart tired of hating cannot learn to love!'

Do you want your fatherland to win or lose? It seems a strange question to ask someone who loves their country; but when it concerns a state that has spent centuries letting neither its own nor other people live, it turns out not to be strange at all.

The fatherland. The country of your birth. The land of your fathers. Andrei Chikatilo, a notorious serial killer, was also a father. Maybe not even a bad one. At home, he was a perfectly normal family man. But Chikatilo murdered dozens of people. How should his son feel about him? My fatherland has killed millions upon millions of people, the children of foreign nations as well as its own – more, even, of its own. And it hasn't stopped killing yet. What are you supposed to think of it?

At a peace conference in Switzerland, Mikhail Bakunin once described 'the soul of the Russian Revolution' this way: 'I am not interested in the opinion of narrow-minded patriots with a thirst for glory. I, a Russian, have publicly and indefatigably protested against the existence of the Russian empire in and of itself. I wish every manner of humiliation and defeat on this empire, because I believe that its victories and glory are, and always will be, grossly inconsistent with the happiness and freedom of the Russian and non-Russian peoples who are its victims and slaves.' He continued, 'Because I see the Russian army as the basis of the empire's power, I here want to publicly express my desire that it will suffer nothing but defeats in any war waged by the empire.' This attitude, the idea that in a country ruled by despots patriotism means hoping that your country's army should always be on the losing side, is the very opposite of 'state' patriotism.

Of course I want my homeland to win. But what will victory look like? Every victory of Hitler's was a defeat for the German people. Conversely, the fall of Nazi Germany was a great victory for the Germans themselves. For the first time in human history, we saw how a people could be resurrected, and live without fever dreams of war.

Thomas Mann was a patriot because he wanted to see his fatherland defeated. In his radio broadcasts entitled 'German Listeners!', he justified the bombing of Germany thus: 'Two thousand bandits a day flying over this quagmire of lies – there's nothing else for it. This unbridled perfidy, this revolting, stomach-turning treachery, this filthy desecration of words and ideas, this monstrous, sadistic butchering of truth must be annihilated, must be eradicated at any cost and by any means necessary.'

Murderers and fools have speculated far too long with patriotism. I think the Polish intellectual and dissident Adam Michnik defined it best, when he described it as 'the precise measure of shame someone feels for crimes committed in the name of their people'.

'Russian patriots' have accused me of being a Russophobe. I believe that my books constitute an answer to that charge: my novels are my love letter to my monstrous fatherland.

Chapter 10

Either

A long time ago, when Mikhail Gorbachev was still a member of the Politburo, when Boris Yeltsin was still the Party's First Secretary in Sverdlovsk and when KGB officer Vladimir Putin was still fighting dissidents in Leningrad, someone once gave me a book. It was a banned book, and I only had it for two days. It looked like a shoebox. In fact, it *was* a shoebox, and in it lay a pile of photographs. Before the triumphant arrival of photocopiers, this is how they duplicated banned books: you took photos of the individual pages, developed the negatives and then printed the pictures.

The book upset me deeply. It probably made no less an impression on me than Solzhenitsyn's *Gulag Archipelago* or Varlam Shalamov's *Kolyma Tales*. Yet this particular book was not about the annihilation of people, but about nature. It was called *The Destruction of Nature in the USSR*. I grew up in a huge country, where nature had to be tamed. In the Geography department's display case at school, there hung the slogan, 'We must not expect nature to give us things; it is our task to take them' (a quote by Ivan Michurin, plant breeder and national hero under Stalin, who believed that the development of fruit trees could be influenced by external factors – rather than only by Mendel's laws of inheritance – and mistakenly thought that the changes he achieved in his plants would prove hereditary; for Soviet scientists, his word was law, and geneticists were persecuted in his name). Nature, then, was there to be conquered and exploited. No one thought that it might be worth protecting.

If you believed the papers, all was well with Russia's ecology, so it wasn't surprising that the book was banned: it clearly proved beyond any doubt that it wasn't only the people who were sitting in the Gulag in Russia, but nature too. But while a prisoner can always find ways to adapt to any prison, nature cannot. When you're busy staying alive, nature is the last thing on your mind.

In the Soviet Union, everything belonged to the people – according to the constitution, that is. In reality, nothing belonged to us. No one owned anything. Instead, the people were the property of the state, and those who ruled over us were merely supervisors, themselves enslaved to the system. Humanity has long known that slaves take no responsibility for their actions or their lives: *nihil habeo, nihil curo*.

The kolkhoz slaves were alienated from the land, and it didn't matter to them whether something grew in the fields or not. The ruling slaves destroyed nature; they carelessly razed forests, poisoned the rivers with waste water from secret military plants and polluted thousands of square kilometres with radioactive waste, and the people could do nothing but put up with it. Eco-consciousness and a prison mentality are irreconcilable. Without freedom, without the chance to take the initiative, there can be no feeling of responsibility towards the environment. And initiative was something the ulus never allowed: any initiative taken by someone from the 'lowly masses' was punished by the higher ranks. Nature can only be protected by a civil society – ecological problems can only be solved one way: by ending the people's alienation from their state, the place where they live, the administration of their community and their street. Yet the Soviet state did all it could to prevent the emergence of a civil society, and the new Russian state is doing the same now.

The ecological catastrophe that has been going on in Russia for years can't be stopped unless there is a civil society to take a stand. But most inhabitants of this gigantic state, when they learn of the barbaric devastation of their environment, are incapable of active opposition. Eco-activists usually end up in prison, like Yevgeny Vitishko, or are forced into exile, like Yevgeniya Chirikova, the famous defender of Khimki Forest near Moscow – among many others. Alarming news of how nature is being exploited reinforces the general feeling of hopelessness and pessimism. The people feel, as they always have, weak and helpless in the face of all-powerful officials who think only about their wallets, not about raising people's eco-consciousness. Today's Russia is still unfamiliar with the notion of social autonomy that forms the basis of Western civilisation.

Russia has some wonderful nature conservation laws, but no functioning mechanism for their implementation, which requires private initiatives, a civil society and a certain kind of character and culture. When it comes to protecting nature, mere external controls are pointless – the controls have to come from within the people themselves. But Russia is a dangerously explosive mixture of nuclear-age technology and Stone Age morality. Then, too, more immediate problems have pushed ecological issues to the back of people's minds. A people desperately fighting for survival doesn't think about the environment.

Polls show that in the list of key contributors to the fear index, environmental damage ranks below military conflicts, unemployment, price rises, reduced production, corruption, injustice, crime, the widening gap between rich and poor, inadequate medical care and low living standards. The country is committing ecological suicide, and hardly knows it. Russia's vast cities are drowning in their own rubbish. Russia still has no waste sorting or processing infrastructure of the kind long established in the West – all rubbish is simply hauled away to gigantic landfills. Future generations will no doubt be grateful.

For the overwhelming majority of people living in this huge country whose nature is being brutally destroyed, ecological issues are overshadowed by a bigger problem: they are more concerned about human survival than the survival of nature, for in Russia, absurd as it may sound, the human species is dying out. Russia's population is shrinking dramatically: according to the 2010 census, my country has lost 1.6 per cent of its population since the last census in 2002. In eight years, 2.2 million people have disappeared – roughly the combined populations of Cardiff, Belfast, Edinburgh and Sheffield, or more than the entire population of Latvia. Compare this to the US, whose population increased by more than 27 million between 2000 and 2010. Other data are moving in the same direction: in 2017, Russia had 115,000 more deaths than births. That year, 1.42 million children were born, but 1.53 million people died.

In the Russian provinces, medical care is simply catastrophic when compared to western Europe. In the past fifteen years, the state has closed half its hospitals. Russian doctors earn on average €2 an hour – less than a cashier at McDonald's. Russians' life expectancy is much lower than in the West, especially for men. A quarter of all Russian men die before they reach fifty-five. The main cause of death is alcohol, and a large number of accidents are associated with alcohol consumption. The rate of people dying in Russia's streets is four times that in the UK – in Russia, it's 12 per 100,000, in the UK it's 3.

The ultimate reason for the high death rate is not alcohol, but the general depression manifesting itself in Russian society. It isn't vodka that kills people, but the fact that they are gripped by a feeling of helplessness, a sense that there is no justice, no help, no escape. Thinking that you can't control anything, that you'll never be able to lead a dignified life and that there's nothing you can do to change any of it is soul-destroying. Scientists have shown that frustration causes aggression and depression, both in rats and in people. The criminal foundation of life in Russian society is the reason that the country has the largest number of violent deaths in the world. In 2015, the male suicide rate was 13 for the UK and 56 for Russia. Russia leads all kinds of rankings: suicides among both older and younger people, and children; prisoners (750 per 100,000); children abandoned by their parents; traffic accidents and plane crashes; people suffering with mental illness; infringements of political rights and freedoms.

I could go on, but I don't feel like it.

People in the West have no idea how tense the situation really is in Russia. The reality of life in Russia, which is never shown on TV, is beyond most of my readers' conceptual world.

The current situation is strongly reminiscent of events a hundred years ago. On the centenary of the 1917 revolution, the Russian Europeans started up again with the slogan 'We can't go on like this'. The twentieth century has trapped Russian history in a Möbius strip: each time the country tries to establish a democratic republic, to introduce elections and a parliament, it finds itself back in a totalitarian empire. It was thus in 1917, and at the beginning of the 1990s. The problems facing my country in the twenty-first century are the same as before the revolution: a high degree of social injustice, and an oppressive and degrading autocracy.

One of those eternal Russian questions rears its head again: is democracy even possible in this country?

There exists another country – which was closer to Europe than Russia, and spent many years knocking on the EU's door – whose regression into dictatorship provides much food for thought. After the Young Turk Revolution of 1908, Turkey became increasingly Westernised; but all of a sudden, it rejected European values. Even the Turkish men and women who lived in Germany voted for autocracy.

Democracy guarantees protection from arbitrary power – and something like that seems totally impossible in Russia, because arbitrariness is the very point of the ulus's entire power structure. In Russia, power is and always was a one-way street. Any movement in the other direction is harshly punished.

The most important characteristic of a democracy is that its people can replace a government via free and fair elections, but is there a single example from Russian history of a government being replaced via free and fair elections? Putin was put on the throne by Yeltsin's 'family'. Yeltsin's victory against the communist Gennady Zyuganov in the 1996 presidential elections was counterfeit (to the great joy of the democratic public). At which elections was it that the people elected Gorbachev, after the death of Konstantin Chernenko in 1985? Was there a free and fair way to replace Brezhnev, Khrushchev, Stalin or Lenin? Who elected the provisional government in 1917? And the tsar could by definition not be elected – his power was God-given. Russia has never had a legal, democratically elected government.

In the face of this historical legacy a democratic future seems impossible, unless you deal with the past once and for all. In Russia, though, history is instrumentalised by the regime: the latest textbooks present Stalin as a good leader, and any public account of his crimes is scotched. My country is a bad student, especially of history. The Germans diligently studied the topics of 'Dealing with the Past' and 'Processing Guilt', and were able to build a democratically orientated society. Germany had to deal with twelve years of brownshirt dictatorship; Russia still has eight hundred years of ulus to work out. My country still lives in the past, and it won't be able to deal with the past until it has dealt with the present. Germany's acknowledgement of national guilt and repentance (initially in the shape of its total capitulation to the Allies) formed the basis of its new democratic incarnation – as Mann wrote in 'Germany and the Germans', 'Anyone who was born a German [has] something in common with German destiny and German guilt.' Without repentance and without acknowledging its national guilt, there can be no fresh start for Russia. But the country is drifting in an entirely different direction.

In 1990, the government erected the Solovetsky Stone on Lubyanka Square, near the KGB building, as a memorial to the victims of Stalin's dictatorship. The stone came from the Solovetsky Islands in the White Sea, the site of the first major Soviet prison camp. Every year on 29 October, on the Day in Remembrance of the Victims of Political Repression, hundreds of people come to this stone and spend hours reading out the names of those who were killed. It is a small memorial, drawing a few hundred people. Meanwhile, the entire country has become one gigantic memorial to Stalin. There has never been a real de-Stalinisation in Russia, no admission of guilt over the crimes that were committed – the terror, the purges, the Ukrainian Holodomor in which millions starved to death, the military interventions in Hungary, Czechoslovakia and Afghanistan. There have been no Nuremberg trials for the Communist Party, which pursued a decades-long genocide against Russians and other people. You can't secrete goods like that in your backpack and try to smuggle them into a democratic future. Russia has to openly and boldly acknowledge its guilt and ask for forgiveness. When Willy Brandt, the German chancellor, went down on his knees in Warsaw, it was an act far more important for Germans than for the Jews and Poles. When will Russia get down on its knees in Warsaw, Budapest, Prague, Tallinn, Vilnius, Riga, Kyiv or Grozny?

Democracy cannot be achieved by lone wolves. People have to take to the streets en masse. In Russia, however, opposition protests are depressingly small when compared to the size of the country's population. Most of the time, their significance is symbolic more than anything else. That they give the desperate a glimmer of hope, and show them that they are not alone, means a lot. In terms of toppling Putin's pyramid of power, though, it isn't enough.

Western observers assumed that the tangible disaffection brought on by the economic crisis, low oil prices and economic sanctions would trigger mass protests from Russians. But the impoverished populace's mass demonstrations failed to materialise. The protests of the past few years, starting in 2011, have been organised by the new middle classes. Again, it is the well-off, well-educated Russian Europeans who are doing the protesting. It is hard to pretend that this opposition can influence the vast majority of Russians. The murdered politician Boris Nemtsov's eye-opening and highly critical reports and Alexei Navalny's admirable struggle against the kleptocracy have failed. Millions of obedient subjects have surrendered their voices to the state; during Russia's rare sporting victories, they cheer and sing the Stalinist national anthem that unites generations of dictators and slaves. The rapid decline of living standards in Russia will continue to not lead to serious mass protests.

That old Russian saying 'Beat your own people, so that others will fear you' perfectly sums up the reaction of the ulus's leaders to Western sanctions. The first thing they did was ban food imports from countries that imposed sanctions against Russia. Who will ever forget the TV images of tractors destroying mountains of food with their caterpillar tracks? Can you imagine London or Berlin or Paris deciding to ban food imports overnight? There'd be protests the very next day! But what did the Russians do? Well . . . The old Soviet mentality is back, or rather, it never went away. There was a joke doing the rounds back then: during a staff meeting in a factory, the workers are told, 'We've decided that everyone will hang themselves. Any questions?' A hand shoots up. 'Will management provide rope, or do we have to bring one from home?'

You can't blame people for not being willing to protest against indignity and injustice. It takes more than courage to protest. Everyone has a family, children, relatives, loved ones they are responsible for. Every regime and every dictatorship exploits the fact that we feel responsible for the ones we love. It may be easy to sacrifice yourself for a just cause, but it's much harder to sacrifice yourself if it means sacrificing your loved ones too. We are the hostages of the people we love, and we will tolerate all manner of degradation to protect them. It is not always a question of risking being arrested for your convictions and going to prison – even the prospect of losing your job forces you to make the tough choice between your dignity and feeding your children. Real enslavement is always a little bit voluntary.

The regime doesn't need the well-off, self-confident middle classes; on the contrary, beggars and have-nots who depend entirely on handouts from the state in the shape of minute wages make the best subjects. These people, who today form the overwhelming majority of voters, willingly go to the jingo-istic government events which employees of state and regional corporations are forced to attend, and they also guarantee high voter turnout. The regime needs an impoverished populace that it can easily manipulate. A well-off population would only cause problems for the Kremlin. When you're starving you're busy thinking of your daily bread – you don't march through the streets for regime change.

Russia is missing one thing which is key to any democratic civil society: citizens. Responsible citizens don't appear overnight; they have to be raised from the bottom up, with the help of initiatives. Yet the state is stifling the emergence of just such an enterprising citizenry any way it can. Officials regard any activist who acts autonomously as a threat, and stifle any initiative that the state hasn't already lanced. The regime defends itself as best it can, and stakes its existence on the second – tame and submissive – head of the conjoined Russian twin. And the idea of democracy is still alien to that head. As Cicero is supposed to have said, 'A slave doesn't dream of being free, but of having his own slaves.' He said it while living in a society that included free people as well as slaves. But climbing the ulus's social ladder doesn't even win you a promotion to slave owner – it only gets you as far as supervisor.

For democratic change to happen in Russia would require a critical mass of self-confident citizens with 'European' values, but the ulus is in the habit of reducing the number of those phoenix-like Russian Europeans, whether by violent or moderate methods. In the course of the twentieth century, the country's elite was either destroyed or forced into exile: millions emigrated after the civil war, and the educated classes practically disappeared; Stalin's purges erased the most skilled and committed elements of the population; and since the 1970s, a continuous stream of émigrés has left first the Soviet Union and then Russia, chiefly experts in technology and science, i.e. the educated elite, who have subsequently joined the ranks of the elite in the US and other states. One name is enough to demonstrate what the Russian brain drain means: Sergey Brin, the founder of Google, was born in Moscow.

In the past few years, the number of people who are leaving Russia has grown rapidly. According to official Russian statistics, about 100,000 people leave each year. But this statistic ignores so-called silent emigration: because the borders are open, people are travelling to Western countries while remaining registered in Russia. Most are scientists, entrepreneurs, lawyers, experts in every conceivable field. They see no future for themselves and their children in Russia. This mass exodus (particularly since the start of the war in Ukraine) has made those who remain only more depressed.

The horrors of the twentieth century have left the country suffering emotionally and mentally. Russia is profoundly depressed. The radio station Echo Moscow, the opposition's chief source of information, once conducted an online poll asking people whether they believed that a dignified life was possible in Russia, or whether they were thinking of emigrating. Eighty per cent of respondents said they were prepared to migrate to the West and no longer believed that it would ever be possible to live a dignified life in Russia.

Russia is failing to produce a new elite; Russian universities are merely training academics destined for the West. Gifted students continue their education abroad, and never come back. They don't believe there is any prospect of fulfilling their potential at a Russian university or academic institute. The level of culture and education is decreasing from year to year, because millions of tertiary educated émigrés, i.e. the potential citizens of a prospective democratic Russia, are being replaced with millions of migrants from Central Asia and the Caucasus, who often lack any education at all. The government helps these people, who speak only little Russian, to settle in the country, and they later become the regime's obedient voters. The abyss between the two Russias is deepening.

In the Soviet Union, your nationality was listed under the infamous 'point five' in your passport. Members of minorities changed their nationality whenever they could. By law, your father's nationality was listed on your birth certificate and included in all other official files relating to you, such as the school register and your medical ID card held by the polyclinic. So if your mother was Russian and your father Jewish, for example, your nationality was registered as 'Jewish'. However, at the age of sixteen, when you got your first domestic ID (a kind of passport), you could freely choose either of your parent's nationality; and because Jews were excluded from many universities and jobs, it was a good idea to change your entry under that 'perilous point five', unless you were planning to emigrate to Israel. In the Soviet empire, being Russian was an ethnic concept as well as a declaration of loyalty, which is why many people from the more than a hundred national minorities living on the Russian Federation's territory changed their 'point five' nationality. A Russian democracy will have to resolve the question of nationality too, and there is currently no prospect of that happening. By encouraging Russian chauvinism, the regime merely keeps tightening this problematic knot.

In political terms, Russian ethnicity was an uncertain construction. At the first opportunity to leave their homeland, Russians started scouring archives for the birth certificates of their German and Jewish great-grandparents, so that they might get rid of their 'Russianness'. Now, the survival instinct of the Soviet forebears who used Russian citizenship as a shield has proved troublesome for their descendants, and should the Russian Federation ever fall apart, the Bashkir, Khanty, Komi, Karelian, Khaka, Kalmyk and dozens of other ethnicities' elites will in all likelihood quickly recall their roots.

Russia's current ethnic make-up makes democracy impossible. The empire of peoples is an atavism. Russia is heavily pregnant with new nation states, just as Yugoslavia once was. The partial collapse of the Russian prison of nations will continue, and wars won't be able to stop it.

Will the Russian democrats – the opposition which is already making plans for the post-Putin era – hear the voices of the Moscow ulus's oppressed peoples? Will they be willing to dissolve the Russian Federation?

The author Volodymyr Vynnychenko, one of the founding fathers of independent Ukraine, famously said in 1919 that 'the Russian democrat ends where the question of Ukraine begins'. I fear that this is true not only of Ukraine, but of all other ethnicities who want to flee the Russian prison. In a famous interview with the *New Times* (NT), Mikhail Khodorkovsky, the great hope of the Russian democratic opposition, declared that he'd be personally willing to go to war to preserve 'Russian' territories:

NT: And the North Caucasus?

MK: ... No problem is more dangerous than the question of territorial integrity. I believe splitting off the North Caucasus would mean something like two million casualties, something like that. I think the war is very bad, but if the choice is between the North Caucasus splitting off and war, then it has to be war ... If you're asking me whether or not I would personally go to war, then yes, I would ... It's our land. We conquered it.

It looks like the empire's curse will hold even democrats in its thrall for a long time to come. Democracy does not need greatness, historical or territorial. But this simple idea hasn't yet entered the consciousness of the Russian opposition. So nowadays, too, a Russian democrat always ends where the Ukrainian, Caucasian, Siberian, etc. question begins.

A further obstacle stands in the way of building a wonderful future Russia: those who are in power will fight to the last to avoid being deposed. The people who seized power in the Kremlin thought they had taken a whole country hostage, but as it turns out, they are their own hostages, hostages of their own power. In recent years, Russian politics has been rooted in the fear of a lonely old man who knows exactly what lies in store for a dictator. He knows that retiring with honours is a luxury he can no longer afford. A usurper with a pension is nonsensical – at best, he can expect prison. An end like Gaddafi's is not inconceivable. This is why he has to fight to the bitter end to retain power, whatever it may cost him. And he knows that enemies and wars are a dictator's elixir of life. People's lives, though, whether they are Russians, Ukrainians, Syrians or any other nationality, don't count.

How free is a Great Khan in such a situation? As free as any hostage. The strongest man in Russia is a slave to the system that once brought him, a former little KGB careerist, to the top of the pyramid of power. He can't afford to give way and implement real reforms, because it would guarantee him a future in prison. Any step towards democracy would ultimately and inevitably lead to regime change.

All the king's men share his fear. The bulldogs under the Kremlin's rug occasionally show their face, and then hide it again. No one knows what goes on there. The only thing that's clear is that all those rival 'Kremlin towers' (this is what Russians call the various clans in the Kremlin) need personal guarantees for themselves and their children. Perhaps the clans are desperately wondering who would be the better guarantor of their existence and wealth: a Putin who is in good health and lives many more years, or a Putin who is shackled. But it's already too late for the retinue to get rid of the man on the throne. The devoted boyars would love to sell their tsar out, but only he can guarantee their privileges. Regime change is too risky for the top brass, because it could mean losing everything their power has won them. Putin's fall might trigger a chain reaction, and he could take many a henchman down with him. The living Great Khan is the only insurance policy those closest to him have.

Thanks to the failed 'White Revolution' in Moscow in 2011, the state is terrified of a Russian Maidan. The protests were peaceful and naive, and the people ingenuously believed that the thieves in charge would be pragmatic enough to enter into a dialogue with the opposition. After all, the millions they had stolen from the people would allow them a happy retirement on the Côte d'Azur or in London. But the man in the Kremlin made his decision when he had the result of the spring 2012 elections falsified: he would rather persevere to the bitter end. It was the point of no return. The Maidan uprising in Kyiv a year and a half later only sped up Russia's evolution into a police state.

This fear of a new people's revolution sometimes takes on a grotesque guise. In the West, the centenary of the Russian Revolution was commemorated with exhibitions and events, but in Russia even the word 'revolution' was banished from public discourse. On 7 November, TV schedules were packed with entertainment programmes that had nothing to do with what was one of the key dates in Russian history. Before that, the people were shown TV series that depicted the Russian Revolution as the result of a sordid conspiracy of Jews and

German agents. They imposed a clear analogy on viewers: these days, the protests in the streets were being orchestrated by US agents.

Instead of commemorating the revolution, Russia commemorates the Great Patriotic War. On 7 November 1941, a military parade took place in Red Square, and the tanks drove directly from the parade into battle against Germany. The anniversary of this event is celebrated with more pomp and circumstance each year. Nowadays, they stage a re-enactment of the 7 November 1941 military parade in Red Square. Any memory of the revolution has been erased from public consciousness.

The state is preparing for an acrimonious fight with its own people. In 2016, they created the Rosgvardiya, a special army tasked to suppress social and political unrest in the country. These troops have unequivocally been given licence to shoot into crowds. When the head of the president's bodyguard was named the Rosgvardiya's commander, state security fused with the personal security of the Great Khan.

Things will proceed according to a tried and tested strategy: the people must be protected from fresh acts of terror, bombings, catastrophes and wars threatening the country. The *siloviki* will do everything they can to spread fear, because a fearful people is easier to rule – and there is much the *siloviki* can do. The secret services have a whole palette of dangers at their fingertips, and the people naturally want to be protected. The moment there's another explosion on the metro in a Russian city, another fire at a nursery school where children lose their lives or another attack at an open-air concert, resulting in hundreds of mutilated casualties, the country's browbeaten voters will voluntarily hand the state a universal letter of indulgence without an end date.

The blind panic created by the prospect of a revolution has mutated into a phobia of any kind of modernisation. The top brass want to maintain the status quo, and fear change full stop. They want time to stand still. But the government's supposed stability rests on the highly unstable foundation of the life of a single individual. Putin will go one way or another, politically or biologically, and the vertical of power needs the ulus to survive the Great Khan's departure at all costs. Special Operation Successor is in full swing already. But the Great Khan isn't looking for a successor. On the contrary, any pretender to the throne is sidelined. Sooner or later, we will find out what exactly happened during this top-secret power struggle – or maybe not.

Is there anyone who can lead Russia into a democratic future? The democratic opposition is fractured and unpopular among most Russians. It is painful to see how incapable leading protesters are of showing solidarity, and instead throw a spanner in each other's works at every election. They simply cannot find a way to work together and present a unity opposition candidate. Each of them wants to be the only shepherd leading the flock. Politicians like that can't hope to win even the fairest of elections.

Furthermore, the opposition is entirely under the Kremlin's control. When the Kremlin is disposed to allow opposition, an opposition exist; when it isn't, then, well, there is no opposition. When the Kremlin wants to throw an opposition leader in jail, that is where they sit; when it doesn't, they are at liberty – temporarily. The opposition is forced to play by the rules laid down by the regime. This cat-and-mouse game could go on and on, and the end result won't necessarily be a free and democratic society.

But how are the democrats meant to achieve power in the first place? There are only two possibilities: free elections or a mass uprising. As everyone knows, there is not and never will be such a thing as elections in Russia, and everyone is scared of uprisings, the Kremlin as well as the democratic opposition. Here, I must quote Pushkin's prophetic lines in full: 'God spare us from Russian revolt, senseless merciless Russian revolt. Those who plot impossible, sudden revolutions in Russia are either young and ignorant of our people or else hard-hearted men who care not a straw about either their own lives or the lives of others.'*

The opposition wants a change of regime and a new man in the Kremlin, but all the while ignores the key issue: regardless who ascends to the Moscow throne, their cap will be the real ruler. The ulus is ruled by power as such. In this historical drama, the Great Khan is but a character, albeit the principal part – and although every actor who fills it contributes something personal,

---

* Alexander Pushkin, *The Captain's Daughter*, trans. Robert Chandler and Elizabeth Chandler (New York: New York Review Books, 2014), p. 130.

a quirk, to the spectacle, and interprets the role of the ruler in a new way, they can change neither the words nor the action of the play. Russia does not need a new actor in the leading role, Russia needs a new play.

To the question 'Quo vadis, Russia?' there aren't all that many answers. Opposition leaders regularly congregate at various forums and conferences (for instance the Free Russia Forum in Vilnius) to work on plans for the country's future transformation into a democracy. Their plans are wonderful. The free Russia of the future will start with free elections. But who will implement them, and what will be the terms? The same tens of thousands of trembling teachers who are currently helping to manipulate Russia's election results? Will there be free elections in Chechnya, under Ramzan Kadyrov? And if there were to be a truly free election in Russia, can we be sure that it will be won by the 'traitor of the people' from the opposition, not by the patriot who fought 'Ukrainian fascists' in Donbas?

Just like totalitarianism, democracy is not something you can proclaim with a decree. Both can only be brought about by a common effort on the part of society as a whole. In Putin's Russia, the people could easily be removed from the levers of power because they never had control over them in the first place. The people don't know that you can and must control your government. It isn't in their genes. A populace that hopes for a benevolent tsar can't be turned into responsible voters overnight. People with a liberal, Western attitude are but a small minority in Russia, and democracy can't happen without a critical mass of citizens, without a mature citizenry.

You can come up with great laws and even enact them, but who will implement them? Who will make democratic reform a reality? Whatever happens, the officials who have blotted their copybook under Putin's regime with corruption and crime must not be part of the creation of the new state. The opposition is demanding a Russian 'Nuremberg' – but who will organise the trials and see them through? Who will deliver the great 'dealing with the past'? Who will uncover the crimes and punish the guilty? What will happen to the thousands of judges who are sacked for passing judgements on the regime's say-so, the tens of thousands of corrupt police officers and the hundreds of thousands of teachers who participated in electoral fraud? You can depose Putin and replace him, but how do you replace millions of corrupt officials, mercenary police officers and malleable judges overnight? There is simply no one to replace them with. You can't replace my vast country's entire population.

Reform won't happen without a proper clean-up of the entire state. Otherwise we will be back in the 1990s, when they made the mistake of retaining the Soviet party and the Soviet state's *nomenklatura*, integrating them into the new state apparatus and thereby preventing Russia from becoming a true democracy. You can't just install an update; you have to replace the entire operating system of the Russian state. But the country isn't a computer, it is inhabited by living, breathing people.

From the magnificent scale drawings of Russia's democratic future, there wafts the scent of utopia.

You don't need a magic telescope to see Russia's immediate future: elections or no elections, constitutional change or Duma decree – the Great Khan will hang on in the Kremlin to the bitter end, his finger on the red button. It no longer matters to those in power whether the people are silent or cheer. And not for the first time, the people will put up with it.

The regime is trying its utmost to preserve the country's status quo, but the preserve will soon reach its use-by date. Stagnation drains more energy from the state than natural evolution.

The worn-out organism needs a fresh injection of patriotism. The logic of war follows its own rules; continuing confrontations with the West and Russia's increasing isolation mean that the coming years will no doubt witness fresh military conflicts and regional wars. The regime will keep pursuing its 'sharp-elbow politics', endure behind its nuclear shield and occasionally poison the world with Novichok. But it can't go on for ever. In this new Cold War, Russia doesn't stand a chance. It's too late to fix the technological deficit. The country is incapable of developing either its own computers or its own cars. In the age of Elon Musk, the Moscow ulus is producing deep-sea satellites (most of its satellites never make it into space, and fall into the ocean). The regime is 'modernising' the country by turning it into a massive fuel pump.

States emerged at a time when the chief source of wealth was land, when territory had to be conquered and defended. Nowadays, the world's chief source of wealth is human intellect: countries are nourished by the likes of Bill Gates, Mark Zuckerberg, Sergey Brin and Elon Musk, and if a state behaves badly, they can move their immense riches somewhere else. This is why modern states don't see any point in territorial expansion. What is important to them is getting the best out of the intellect of free human beings.

The Bolsheviks once abolished the thirteen-day time gap between tsarist Russia and the West by decree, but a decree won't help Russia catch up with the new era of technology, which values people above all else and whose developments are driven by individual rights and freedoms.

The country has been robbed of its future. The ulus doesn't envisage a future. No one can deny the feeling of hopelessness in Russian society. Knowing that there is nothing you can do to change life in Russia has thrown the country into a depression that – aside from brief fits of patriotic hysteria during big sporting events – just keeps on growing.

Which scenario will history choose for Russia now? There is zero hope that the country will be saved by a Russian Stauffenberg plot, an Operation Valkyrie organised by those close to the Great Khan. In Nazi Germany, there were still people in the military with their own conceptions of honour and patriotism, but today's Russian 'elite' simply isn't an environment where such a conspiracy could take root and grow. There'll be no Valkyries flying into the Kremlin.

The Moscow ulus's pyramid of power is a sturdy structure. Its one inherent defect is that when the time comes for the throne to change hands, the whole construction will start wobbling. No one can predict how the power struggle between the rival clans will end, but we can be sure that the day will come, and that the successor will have their work cut out.

When the balance of power tips, the colossal criminal pyramid will inevitably implode, burying the entire country under its rubble. The empire's partial collapse will continue at full throttle. The first to leave the sinking ship will be Chechnya. The Caucasian republic has only remained part of the Russian Federation thanks to the close relationship of two khans and the huge amount of protection money that Russia is paying Chechnya.

The empire of the tsars dissolved within a few months. The Soviet Union broke up in three days. The Putinist 'vertical of power' will fall apart in a matter of hours. After Chechnya, other North Caucasus republics will sever ties with Russia, followed by Tatarstan, Bashkiria and Yakutia, and then the Siberian regions will begin their fight for independence from the centre, with the slogan 'Stop Moscow stealing our natural resources!'

You can see what awaits Russia when you look at Donbas, where the regional mafia are battling it out for control of the region and establishing their criminal regime. It is doubtful that constitutional democracies will be established on the territories that declare their independence from Moscow. Yugoslavia showed how quickly brutal wars and ethnic cleansing can start up in a multinational state, and if violence escalates my country will regress hundreds of years. For the West, it would mean a fresh wave of countless refugees. There will soon be a fresh era of turmoil in Russia, where democratic ideas are rejected by the general population and the people put their hopes in a strongman. A strongman will surely be found, and the West, too, will understand and accept a 'dictatorship of order'. No one wants turmoil in a country with a red button but no master.

The integrity of the Russian Federation is as much of an illusion and a lie as the integrity of the Soviet republics once was. Gorbachev's aim was to prevent the Soviet Union from falling apart, which is why, on 17 March 1991, he conducted the only referendum in Soviet history, asking the people whether they wanted the Soviet Union to remain a unified state. The 'yes' vote won with 70.2 per cent in Ukraine, 82.7 per cent in Belarus, 93.7 per cent in Uzbekistan, 94.1 per cent in Kazakhstan, 93.3 per cent in Azerbaijan, 96.4 per cent in Kyrgyzstan, 96.2 per cent in Tajikistan and 97.9 per cent in Turkmenistan. A few months later, the Soviet empire gave up the ghost, and the unified people turned out to be a sham generated by propaganda. No one protested – in the new republics, they celebrated their yearned-for independence from their 'big brother' with whoops and cheers.

In *Dead Souls* – perhaps the most Russian of all Russian

literary works – Gogol compares my homeland to a speeding troika, which careers along and overtakes other countries: 'Is it not like that that you, too, Russia, are speeding along like a spirited troika that nothing can overtake? ... Russia, where are you flying to? Answer! She gives no answer. The bells fill the air with their wonderful tinkling; the air is torn asunder, it thunders and is transformed into wind; everything on earth is flying past, and, looking askance, other nations and states draw aside and make way for her.'* Every schoolchild knows these famous lines, and they gave generations of Russian readers hope. After all, it has to be speeding somewhere – into a bright future, perhaps?

A century and a half has passed since Gogol, and the country has experienced terrible things – as have people's souls. Communism's epoch-making experiment in social liberation led to an even crueller dictatorship. Sadly, equipped as Russia is with these experiences, Gogol would these days be more likely to compare Russia to a metro train that keeps travelling from one end of the tunnel to the other, from orderly dictatorship to anarchic democracy and back. That is its itinerary, the track it's on, and the train will take you nowhere else.

My generation has travelled through the Russian tunnel in both directions: perestroika and a feeble government brought

---

* Nikolai Gogol, *Dead Souls*, trans. David Magarshack (London: Penguin, 1961), p. 259.

chaos to the country in the 1990s, then the train turned in the opposite direction and we ended up in the Putinist empire.

The next stops along the route have already been announced. Do we really want to go there?

Chapter 11

Or

In the nineteenth century, the poet Fyodor Tyutchev formulated the Russian creed thus: you cannot grasp Russia with your mind – all you can do is have faith in it. Ever since, Russians have repeated this trope like a mantra. Now, in the twenty-first century, the first part of his claim is long outdated; you can, and must, grasp this country with your mind. But even now it still echoes the feelings of any Russian who loves their country despite the 'patriots': you must have faith in Russia.

There is only one reason why democracy can win out in Russia: it must.

Nature has its laws: every river at some point ends in the sea. Human nature has its laws too: once upon a time, they would kill a sick child, and old people who were no use to others, because there was not enough food to go round. That was the norm back then. But humanity evolves according to the law of anthropomorphism: the evolutionary goal of Homo sapiens is to replace primeval aggression, the urge to bag everything, vanquish every enemy, mark every corner and subjugate anyone weaker than you with mercy, empathy, tolerance and a sense of responsibility towards those weaker than you. History has taken us from coarse creature to spiritual and intellectual being and taught us virtues such as mercy, fairness and dignity. Standards change. In the beginning only the strong had rights, but then institutions emerged – and are continuing to emerge – that protect the weak from the strong, and the cruel arbitrariness of autocracy was replaced by states that are subject to the rule of law. Humanity is travelling the long road that leads from bellicose brutality to human kindness and honouring the rights of individuals. Sooner or later, everyone travels down this road. Russia is no exception.

Two attempts to introduce democracy in Russia have failed. But there will surely be further such attempts. The first Russian democracy of 1917 lasted just a few months. The second, in the 1990s, barely managed to cling on for a handful of years. Next time, the 'third Russian democracy' may be able to survive for longer. What is important is that the country breaks its vicious circle of violence and rejects the paradigm of bloodshed. Only a peaceful protest movement can save Russia's future.

The word is the one weapon the new Russian opposition has in its arsenal. The regime has banished the disaffected to the ghetto of the internet, and the ghetto is seething, boiling with rage. In Russia, a war of reason is being fought, and we know who will win. In the battle between dictators and free speech, the word has always emerged the victor – in the old Russian duel between poet and tsar, the latter doesn't stand a chance.

It simply isn't the case that Russians are unfit for democracy. Just like all other people, Russians, too, are capable of living in a democratic society. You need look no further than the millions of Russian émigrés living in the West, who not only easily manage to adapt to democratic norms but often flourish there, thanks to their talent and expertise.

It all depends on a given society's prevailing norms. When norms change, people change. When the German state legalised the persecution of Jews, people were raised within the norms of race laws. In the new German democracy, the norms proscribe anti-Semitism.

In modern Russia, political prisoners, total corruption, fear and the absence of any democratic freedoms are the norm. But social norms don't fall from the sky. They change as people change. We raise ourselves, so to speak, setting our own standards and thereby changing society as a whole.

Revolutions happen because we humans need them to feel human. Otherwise we would never revolt against anything. We need moments such as these in our lives, when we can no longer tolerate the degradation and take to the streets to fight for our human dignity.

In recent times, it has been mainly the young who have protested against the regime. Thousands of schoolchildren and students in Moscow, St Petersburg and other Russian cities are protesting peacefully in the streets. Look at their faces: you will find no sign of despondence, no hopelessness – on the contrary, they radiate self-assurance and confidence. The new generation doesn't watch TV; propaganda doesn't reach them. The young are different. They don't want to suffocate in Putin's mouldy realm. This is another reason to be optimistic: youth ultimately always wins.

Yes, these people are still a minority in Russia. A marginal minority. As yet, they are on the losing side, but they are not afraid of losing. Tolstoy lost too, and so did Rachmaninov, Malevich and the seven brave people who entered Red Square in 1968. They are in honourable company.

Compared to the sluggish masses, the number of opposition activists is very small, and it is confined to Moscow, St Petersburg and a few other large cities. But any historical process is always preceded by an avant-garde. These progressives are ready to fight for democracy, and will take the masses with them. In Russia, fateful events have always happened in the two capital cities.

As of now, these people are still in the minority, but who knows what tomorrow will bring? The rules for deposing an authoritarian regime are the same everywhere: some hundreds of thousands of people in the streets combined with a conspiracy of courtiers, or, alternatively, a million people in the streets – the latter will suffice without a conspiracy.

Who knows what might trigger it. Pension reform? Some 'black swan' or other? More schoolchildren poisoned by noxious fumes from a gigantic landfill nearby, as happened in Volokolamsk in spring 2018, when outraged parents of dozens of poisoned children protested, and the city's entire population suddenly filled the streets? Will there be a 'waste revolution' in Russia? Then, soon, it won't be only the marginalised opposition, but the majority of the country's inhabitants chanting, 'It's our city, our country – and we care!'

Whatever the future may bring, there are already people in Russia today who protest in the streets and squares in defence of their human dignity, and thus the dignity of all humanity. We should do everything we can to support them.

How can Western democracies help these people? Simple: follow the law. The money that flows out of Russia is dirty money. Russia's rulers stole their wealth from the people, full stop. According to the laws of any country that is governed by the rule of law, dirty money must be seized, and the criminals belong in prison. The West needs to talk to Russian kleptocrats in the plain language of the law. The reason it hasn't done so yet is that the sum of money involved is so mind-boggling that it almost leaves you speechless.

Those who enjoy the use of the state's assets don't invest their stolen capital in their own country, but store their swag in the West. The reason is obvious: only in democratic countries are the cash in your bank account and your property investments protected from the whims of the strong by laws and courts. In Russia, stealing money is easy, but it's even easier to lose it.

In the West, laws against money laundering are often side-stepped. Because of the colossal sums involved, it's hard to stay within the bounds of the law and freeze accounts that contain stolen money, and there are enough respectable, honourable people in the world who want to cosy up to Russian money-bags. After all, they have mouths to feed, and laundered money smells less bad. You kiss the hand that feeds you.

It isn't even a question of run-of-the-mill robbery. It is the robbery of the century. One of the world's richest countries has been looted; and given that 'legalising' the ill-gotten gains is a crime perpetrated within the jurisdiction of democratic countries, it should also be punished there. The only effective sanction against this 'robber state' is to freeze and confiscate the loot. Sure, Western lawyers, banks, estate agents and the builders of luxury yachts will see a reduction in their earnings, but democratic societies can easily withstand that sort of thing.

Russia's impending disintegration is causing much consternation, both inside Russia and in the West. But the centrifugal force that is affecting the nations and regions of the last empire in the world is not merely destructive, but a decontaminating, rehabilitating and healing force. The future break-up of the Russian Federation may be painful, but it will be an important and necessary step on the road to democracy. Russian minds have to learn to accept that there can be more than one state where Russian is the official language. The empire has to be removed from minds and souls like a malignant tumour. Only once the operation has been successfully performed will the states that emerge in the former territory of the Moscow ulus be able push through democratic reform.

A democratic Russia on the territory of the fifteenth-century Moscow ulus? It would be a miracle. But who, before the break-up of the Soviet Union, believed that it would dissolve so quickly? Yet the miracle happened. Why shouldn't other miracles be possible? Russia is an odd country, where the most unlikely dreams and predictions come true. Did anyone take Amalrik seriously when he prophesied, back in the 1960s, that the mighty and eternal Soviet empire would vanish so rapidly and ignominiously? Who would have thought that the Soviet army would leave eastern Europe, that Germany's two halves would reunite, that new independent states would appear on the map and embark on the road to the European family of nations? All this goes to prove that miracles are real.

No one can foresee exactly when the miracle will happen. In democratic states, the government is regularly elected anew, and although you know the date of the next general election, you don't know who will win. It's different in Russia: you know exactly who will win the next presidential election, but not where the president will be a month later. Likewise, Putin doesn't know when and how Putin's regime will end, but the end is coming. Even with all its police officers, soldiers, judges and prisons, a dictatorship can't ban the future. The laws of political biology all point towards green, living shoots breaking through the tarmac.

The online opposition station TV Rain live-streams opposition rallies and marches across the country. During the recent mass protests, the police violently crushed a demonstration on Pushkin Square in Moscow. The 'Cosmonauts' – as the OMON units are nicknamed, because of their special gear – hit people with batons, dragged young men and women out of the crowd and manhandled them into vans whose windows were secured with metal grilles. Right in the midst of it all, a journalist tried to speak to some of the people around him. He approached a girl who was about seventeen or eighteen, dressed in jeans and a T-shirt, a teenager like any other:

'Aren't you scared?'

'Yes!' she replied. 'Really scared!'

'Then why are you here?'

'They have taken everything from us in this country, and I came here so that they don't take away my future.'

This girl is Russia's future.

Afterword to the English Edition

I. Waiting for a New Putin

For years, wherever my travels around the world took me, when a cab driver heard that I was Russian they immediately smiled. 'Putin!' they'd say, and give me a thumbs-up. I never understood why cab drivers loved Putin so much. All I knew was that there were two Putins involved. You couldn't love mine – and the cab drivers had created a Putin in their own image.

It's obvious why you would hate my Putin. The KGB agent began his presidential career with the bloody sacrifice of his own people: he blew up Moscow residents in their apartment blocks as a pretext for war with Chechnya. After that, things moved in just one direction: towards the 24 February 2022 invasion of Ukraine. All those years in between, though, there were other Putins being admired by many people around the world.

During the chaotic Russian 1990s, the battered populace was desperate for order to be restored and to see their humiliated fatherland 'rise from its knees'. They hoped for a new ruler with a fist of iron. Generations of slaves had identified with their vast empire, and Putin promised to heal the national wound: the time of chaos was over, and Russia would return to its position at the top of the world.

The propaganda image of the omnipotent ruler and saviour of his people went down well. The evil West wanted to destroy us, and only the good tsar could save our *Russkiy mir*, 'the Russian world'. Crimea's 'restoration' to Holy Russia may not have improved the roads, supplied villages with running water or installed radiators in bathrooms, but it did give people a chance to be proud of their Putin.

The watchword of Putinist ideology is *Russkiy mir*. The word *mir* originally meant a Russian village community, and the mentality of large sections of the Russian population is today still the mentality of a medieval rural community. If someone cried, 'They're beating our people!' everyone would come running out armed with sticks and pitchforks, without stopping to think whether 'our people' were in the right. Thus Putinist propaganda has been crying for years that 'they're beating our people in Ukraine!' This peculiar 'village mentality' also explains why so many Russians who live in the West support

Putin and his war. You may physically live in Zurich, London or Larnaca, but mentally you're in the *Russkiy mir*. As the late actor Sergei Bodrov – a cult figure in Russia (in the blockbuster sequel *Brother 2*, he played a good Russian gangster who goes to the US and kills dozens of Americans) – once said in an interview, 'It's hard to criticise your people in wartime, even if they're in the wrong.'

On Planet Russkiy Mir, Putin has occupied the niche of a good and victorious tsar in the evil West's war against 'our people'. Now, let's consider his place on Planet Earth. The countless professional Putin-apologists in the West who have earned their crust as experts on Russia don't interest me, nor do corrupt politicians – today you're chancellor of Germany, tomorrow you're Putin's lackey. But what needs explaining is why anyone who isn't paid to do so would admire Putin. It is not just online platforms in India or Latin America that depict Putin as a hero who is finally telling the imperialist US that it has overstepped the mark, and not only Iranian and North Korean leaders whose feelings Putin echoed when he famously threw down the gauntlet to the US in Munich in 2007, saying that 'a unipolar world . . . describes a scenario in which there is one centre of authority, one centre of force, one centre of decision-making . . . The world cannot accept such a scenario. It is pernicious, including for the sovereign himself.' The principle that 'the enemy of my enemy is my friend' unites left-wingers and right-wingers across the world.

Western democracies, too, found plenty of reasons to love

Putin. They said the man stood for moral values: Christianity, the institution of the family, the fight against single-sex marriage and 'gay parades'. They admired him for his demonstrative freedom from political correctness and for his open anti-wokeness. He was a truly manly state leader, they said, who represented muscular masculinity and defended the world against 'gender madness'. The 'badass from the east' quietly called Western society in the days of cancel culture into question: 'Why should men be ashamed of being men? Why should white people feel burdened by an "original sin" of racism, just because they are white?' In democratic countries, too, many people were impressed by his macho posturing. Brigitte Bardot considered Putin someone who had done more for nature and animal conservation than all France's presidents rolled into one, others were awestruck when he showed off his strapping naked torso, and the Swiss right-wing populist Roger Köppel pinpointed why the cab drivers of the world admire Putin so much when he said, 'Putin exposes the hollow moralism of his opponents and the decadence of the West.' It looks like the spook with the 'mysterious Russian soul' has been nothing but a mirror reflecting Western desire.

And now Putin's admirers around the world are disappointed. There is no brutal macho sitting in the saddle – just a bloated dwarf who hides behind an infinitely long table. No Western politician has done more for NATO's eastward expansion than Putin. Now, more countries will be eager to join the defence alliance. Instead of saving animals and the environment, he orders cities to be bombed, women to be raped, children to be killed. This is not what moral, Christian family values look like.

The *Russkiy mir* is also deeply disappointed. Only intellectuals are tortured by those accursed Russian questions, 'Who's to blame?' and 'What now?' For ordinary people, the most important of all Russian questions is: 'Is the tsar real or fake?' Victory alone can provide the answer. Stalin was real, and is still revered. Gorbachev, however, lost both the war in Afghanistan and the Cold War against the West, so 'Gorby' was evidently a false tsar, and Russians scorn and loathe him to this day.

By annexing Crimea, Putin legitimised his presidency. In the eyes of the people, he was a real tsar. But the absence of victory in Ukraine is drastically undermining his legitimacy. The Telegram messaging channels run by the 'patriotic opposition', with their hundreds of thousands of followers, are already crying high treason and demanding victory no matter what. The more coffins return from Ukraine, the louder the cry: 'They're beating our people!' The search for a real tsar has already begun.

People are disappointed in the actual man because he was unable live up to his admirers' expectations. The man will disappear, but his worshippers and their expectations will remain. In Russia, the de-Putinisation will be carried out by a new Putin with a different name. In the West, once Putin has disappeared, someone else will have to dazzle people with his macho image and defy US imperialism. After all, someone has to stand up to gay marriage, NATO and US hegemony! Can people really ever be cured of their need for political masculinity?

Putin will disappear, but the desires he has projected will not vanish into thin air with him. The actor who has played all these Putins on the world stage has failed in every regard. The role is now waiting to be filled by someone else.

II. A Letter to Europe, Sent Poste Restante

Dear Europe,

Who are you? What are you? Where are you?

I was born in Europe, but you were always on the other side of the barbed wire. I wanted to read your authors, but many of them were banned over here. I wanted to stroll through your streets, but couldn't reach you. For generations of Soviet people, you were a fairy tale, a myth. Europe is a Russian myth about human life. For those of us who were suffocating behind the Iron Curtain, you embodied 'European' values: the rights of the individual, respect for human dignity, freedom – all the things that we were deprived of.

It is for this Europe that the Ukrainians protested in the Maidan in 2014, for this Europe that the men and women of the 'celestial hundred' lost their lives on the barricades – not for the European Union represented by bureaucrats in Brussels, but for a life at home that was fit for human beings. They rose up against the criminal gang that ruled Ukraine, and which still rules in Russia. Their Europe was synonymous with dignity. And this is precisely what the dictator in the Kremlin cannot forgive, and will never forgive. That is why Russian propaganda is telling Russians that Europe means fascism. The majority of the Russian people has been zombified by TV, and believes that the US and Europe are waging a war whose aim is the destruction of Russia at the hands of the Ukrainian Nazis. According to their world view, Russia is an island surrounded by enemies and Europe is the cradle of fascism, and we, like our grandfathers before us, must defend our homeland against them. Propaganda lies, but lies are a highly effective weapon. Dear Europe, you can't even imagine hating Russia with a passion and wanting nothing more than to destroy Russia.

Of course none of it is true. But what is the truth?

Think back to the last few pre-war years (which is what they will call the early twenty-first century in future). You were ill, exhausted by financial problems, conflicts and crises, tired of being dominated by bureaucracy. You were the Europe of officials who told farmers what they should plant in their fields and how, a Europe choked by waves of refugees from Asia and Africa. You were a Europe that countries wanted to leave. And then, to top it all, Covid came along, followed by closed borders and draconian measures. You self-isolated and waited for 'normal' life to finally return. After the pandemic came the war.

We notice the air only when it runs out. European values are the air that you breathe. If Europeans didn't realise how truly blessed they were in the last pre-war years – blessed with freedom, constitutional rights, democracy, the separation of powers, an independent judiciary, free and unfalsified elections – it means that things weren't going all that badly. Because then war arrived, and now, dear Europe, you suddenly feel like yourself again, you have found yourself again: in the face of a common threat, you came together, felt solidarity, realised that you needed to protect your freedom, your communal home, your dignity, the things you don't want to give up, everything you live for, everything that makes you Europe.

In 2014, Ukraine said, *'Je suis Europe.'* You said nothing. And now, as Russian missiles destroy Ukrainian cities, as Russian soldiers loot, rob, rape and murder, you have finally replied: *'Je suis Ukraine.'*

It is as if you have been roused. You have woken up. For so many years, you were entangled hand and foot in the threads of Putin's gas pipelines. Putin has made you need his oil like a drug addict. Dirty money from Russia, stolen from the people by Putin's regime, has infected your banks, your economy and your politicians.

Corrupt experts say: We must understand Putin and his mysterious Russian soul, and we have to make concessions! Sanctions are a bad idea, because they'll hit us Europeans the hardest! Americans are trying to drive a wedge between us and the Russians! We need jobs, gas and peace! And by the way, maybe Putin is right, and there really are Nazis in power in Ukraine? We need peace!

Your experts, dear Europe, have betrayed you – and now we are at war.

The war has changed you, it has made you what you really are: unified, strong and humane. You are welcoming millions of Ukrainian women and children. You are forgoing the dirty money with which Putin's regime is financing the killings. You are showing solidarity with the Ukrainians who are fighting for 'your and our freedom', for their and our future, for the dignity of Europe and all humankind.

Dear Europe, in these difficult days and weeks you have become yourself. I see you in the squares of your cities. People who protest against war and defend human kindness have wonderful, beautiful faces.

What is important to me is that, even after the war, after our common victory, you remain united, strong, wise, young and beautiful, that you acknowledge your mistakes and put things right, that you keep remembering who you are and what you want.

I don't know if you will read this letter. But I am writing it anyway, and will send it to be left till called for.

I know that only unwritten letters never arrive.

Index